Utah's Secret Combinations

2022 Edition

Defending Utah

The text in this book is copyrighted by Deseret Family Learning, LLC / Defending Utah.

FAIR USE NOTICE: All images in this book are included for educational purposes and journalistic commentary in accordance with the Fair Use clause of the United States copyright code. While your purchase of this book is purchasing the copyrighted text, use of fair-use photos is for reference regarding journalistic commentary.

The copyright for each image is listed individually as follows:

Figure 1: Custom art with photo from unsplash.com, used according to license
Figure 2: Custom made chart
Figure 3: The People's Party of Utah, Public domain, via Wikimedia Commons
Figure 4: Screenshot of slcfr.org, via fair-use
Figures 5 - 8: Screenshot of sltrib.com, via fair-use
Figure 9: Screenshot of newsbreak.com, via fair-use
Figure 10: Screenshot of Daily Utah Chronicle, University of Utah school newspaper, 2018, via fair-use
Figure 11: Utonian image scan, page 172, 1920, public domain
Figure 12: Public Twitter post, via fair-use
Figure 13: See link online
Figures 14 - 15: KSL screenshots, via fair-use
Figure 16: UtahPolicy.com Screenshot, via fair-use
Figure 17: Public Twitter post, via fair-use
Figure 18: Public Twitter post, via fair-use
Figure 19: Public Twitter post, via fair-use
Figure 20: Public Facebook post, via fair-use
Figures 21-22: Scan of old, out-of-print, pamphlets, via fair-use
Figures 23 - 34: - Public Domain Content

Table of Contents

Figure 1

Introduction – Part I

This book has been made possible by the contributions of countless Defending Utah member volunteers giving hundreds of consecrated hours of their time and donations over nearly a decade.

Defending Utah has published much over the years on the subject of conspiracy on our various media channels. Our ever-improving liberty "boot camp" on our website takes you from a basic foundation to understanding that conspiracies are not only real, but that they shape the history of the world. They influence greatly how all people see the world. This book is presented to you, not as an introduction to the concept of conspiracies, but to take your understanding to the next level.

We speak mostly from an LDS perspective because we are based in Utah where we have traced the history of conspiracy, and where the LDS perspective is simply a part of this history. But please understand very well that this same story, based on the same principles, plays out all around the world, adapted to the culture and circumstances of each local culture.
It is impossible to truly tell this story at this depth without picking a local culture and including it in the discussion.

In understanding the tense of this book, we generally refer to "us," "we" and "our" as either "all of us Utahns" or as "all of us members" of Defending Utah that are considering the history of the state of Utah that we all live in. We generally refer to the LDS church organization in third person, and we may also sometimes speak as being LDS ourselves or as being Utahns in general with no denomination. No specific meaning should be taken from the changing of this perspective from time to time. This book is intended to help all people understand principles, understand the conspiracy, and live free, whether you're religious or not.

If you have not yet come to the realization that a vast conspiracy is working to take over the freedom of all lands, nations, and countries, then please first take advantage of many who have done the work to lay the foundation of exposing this international conspiracy from books like, "None Dare Call It Conspiracy" (recommended by Ezra Taft Benson), "The Naked Capitalist," and "Shadows of Power" to name just a few. Those are efforts we would not attempt to replicate and encourage you to start with these first.

Introduction – Part II

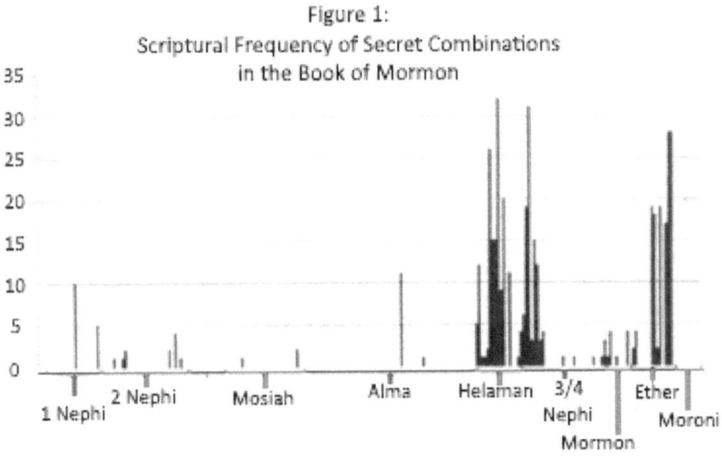

Figure 2

The subject of Secret Combinations in the Book of Mormon occurs an average of every 1.2 pages of text. There are some 442 verses that, in their context, deal with this topic. In fact, the topic of Secret Combinations is mentioned more than any other subject apart from our Savior and His Atonement for us.

In making the record of the Jaredite people and the Secret Combinations among them, Moroni takes some time out to speak directly to us in **our day**. He says,

> *Wherefore, O ye Gentiles, it is wisdom in God that these things should be shown unto you, that thereby ye may repent of your sins, and suffer not that these murderous combinations shall get*

above you, which are built up to get power and gain — and … the sword of the justice of the Eternal God shall fall upon you, to your overthrow and destruction if ye shall suffer these things to be. (Ether 8:23)

Some people ask the questions:

- Why even talk about the conspiracy?
- Doesn't that just give them power?
- Shouldn't we ignore them and just "focus on the positive"?

Moroni makes it clear that these questions are misguided when he explained why he was telling us in the last days about the modern conspiracy,

> *Wherefore, I, Moroni, am commanded to write these things that evil may be done away, and that the time may come that Satan may have no power upon the hearts of the children of men.* (Ether 8:26)

Understanding how Satan (tyranny) works, and living accordingly, removes his power!

The ancient Chinese general Sun Tzu explained the efficacy of this principle when he taught,

> *If you know the enemy and know yourself, you need not fear the result of a hundred battles. If you know yourself but not the enemy, for every*

victory gained you will also suffer a defeat. (Art of War)

Brigham Young tried to help us understand this as well when he said,

> *We should not only study good, and its effects upon our race, but also evil, and its consequences.* (Journal of Discourses 2:94)

We also read in the Doctrine and Covenants that,

> *We should waste and wear out our lives in bringing to light all the hidden things of darkness, wherein we know them; These should then be attended to with great earnestness.* (123:13-14)

A major branch of the grand earthly conspiracy of Satan in our day is found in Communism. In January of 1950, the First Presidency of The Church of Jesus Christ of Latter-day Saints issued a proclamation opposing Communism saying,

> *No member of this Church can be true to his faith, nor can any American be loyal to his trust, while lending aid, encouragement, or sympathy to any of these false philosophies; for if he does, they will prove snares to his feet.* (Official pamphlet printed by Deseret Book and distributed by the Church Home Teaching program. See Appendix A)

Hundreds of quotes from Utah leaders, like the one following, have supported this in great detail for decades:

> *On the flyleaf of the book, The Naked Communist, by W. Cleon Skousen, we find this quotation, (and I admonish everybody to read that excellent book of Chief Skousen's) : 'the conflict between communism and freedom is the problem of our time. It overshadows all other problems. This conflict mirrors our age, its toils, its tensions, its troubles, and its tasks. On the outcome of this conflict depends the future of mankind.* (President David O. McKay, Conference Report, Oct 1959, pg. 5)

Introduction – Part III

The Communist Manifesto was co-written by Karl Marx. While employed by a group called the League of Just Men. The League of Just Men changed its name to the Communist League after the publication of Marx's Manifesto. But to trace the origins of this we must go back further. Who or what was the League of Just Men? We go back further still, and for purposes of clear continuity in history, we stop in 1776 at one of the most amazing coincidences in all of history. Not July fourth, and our Declaration of Independence, but May first of 1776.

On this day, a Conspiracy to rule the world, called the Illuminati, was established in Bavaria by a man named Adam Weishaupt. Weishaupt had coalesced into a single organization many of the existing Conspiracies of the day. His brilliance was obvious in just the organization of the Illuminati, with concentric circles of power, influence, and knowledge of the ultimate goal. This enabled the Conspiracy to use the energies and talents of many who knew not for whom or for what they were laboring.

The Goals of the Illuminati, as found in Dr. John Robison's 1798 exposé, "Proofs of a Conspiracy," have been summarized as follows:

1. Obliteration of Christianity
2. Promotion of Sensuality
3. Taking Away of Private Property
4. Abandonment of all Religion and Morality
5. Rejection of Marriage
6. Government Take Over of Parenting
7. Business Licensing
8. Wrecking of Civilization and giving over of society to general plunder (taxing)
9. Political Degeneracy
10. Manipulation of the people's thinking
11. Promotion and committing evil for the sake of evil

It should be obvious that this is the agenda of statists of all stripes today: Communist, Fascist, Socialist, Progressive, etc.

The Illuminati succeeded very quickly in penetrating the academic communities at the universities in Germany. They succeeded in infiltrating and then taking over, for their purposes, certain lodges of the Masonic Order in France. The Illuminati was primarily responsible for the French Revolution, and the terror from which France has never really recovered.

In the same year as Dr. Robison's book, Abbe Baruel, a French priest, published a scholarly four-volume work exposing the Illuminati. And in our own country, President George Washington wrote to friends warning of the existence of the Illuminati and its potential threat to the united States.

John Adams understood this conspiracy and worked to expose the organization and its agenda. He shared Dr. Robison's book far and wide. In a letter to his wife on the 28th of May 1798,

> *To destroy and undermine Religion has been the chief engine in the accomplishment of this mighty Revolution throughout Europe. We have felt no small share of the bale full influence of the Age of Reason, but to have a thorough Idea of the deep-laid system, you must read a work lately published called "Proofs of a Conspiracy against all the Religions and Governments of Europe," by John Robison, Professor of Natural Philosophy in the university of Edinburgh.' This Book I have sent to Dr. Belknap with a request that if he possessed a Copy, that he would send it to Mr. Cranch. If he has not, he will lend it to him. You will read the book with astonishment.* (founders.archives.gov /documents/Adams/04-13-02-0023)

To hide their efforts, the Illuminati organization was made up of levels within levels. The entry level being people that neither understood that there were levels within the organization, nor their ultimate goals. They would prove themselves to their superiors who would then bring them up the ranks of the organization until they proved their loyalty to the organization's Satanic agenda.

The organizational structure and goals of the Illuminati were discovered when one of their couriers was struck by lightning. The Bavarian government gained possession of the Illuminati's documents-in-transit thus outlawing the Illuminati and Weishaupt was forced to feign repentance. In these documents, Bavarian officials discovered the inner workings of the Illuminati including their structure. To protect the ultimate goals of the Illuminati as a secret, the organization was separated into levels, and levels within levels.

Entry level members of the organization were not privy to the Illuminati's ultimate goals of the destruction of religion and national sovereignty. These levels didn't even know there were levels to the organization until they had proven themselves to their superiors and were invited to ever ascending ranks within the order. These ranks are reported to have changed from time to time but are traced somewhat in John Robison's book. Two other sources more specifically outline the ranks as follows:

From
"Recess among the Aeropagites" 12/20/1781

Minerval:
Novice,
Minerval,
Illuminatus minor/Minerval illuminatus
Blue Masonry:
Apprentice,
Fellow Craft,
Master
Mysteries Class:
Illuminatus Major/Scottish Novice,
Illuminatus Dirigens/ Scottish Knight
Greater Mysteries Class:
Priest,
Magus,
Regent

From
"Convention of Munich" 3/21/1782

Final Degree System of the Illuminati Order.

I. Preparatory Class
1. Novice.
2. Minerval.
3. Illuminatus Minor. Lesser Illuminati.

II. Freemasonic Class
1. Apprentice – Fellowcraft – Master. (Symbolic Freemasonry).
2. Illuminatus Major. Greater Illuminati or Scottish Novice.
3. Illuminatus Dirgens. Scottish Knight.

III. Mysteries Class
1. Lesser Mysteries
a) Presbyter. Priest.
b) Regent or Princeps. Prince.

2. Greater Mysteries
a)Magus or Philosophus. Magician or Philosopher.
b) Rex or Doceten. King or Docetist(1).

After Weishaupt's fake repentance, with their leader forced underground, the inner circle of the Illuminati relentlessly remained undeterred in achieving their goals.

In the 1780s the **Jacobin** club was formed to implement the agenda started by Weishaupt and the Illuminati.

George Washington, in a letter to Reverend GW Snyder understood the inseparable nature of the two organizations when he said,

> *It was not my intention to doubt that the doctrine of the Illuminati, and the principles of*

Jacobinism, had not spread in the United States. On the contrary, no one is more satisfied of this fact than I am.
(September 25, 1798
loc.gov/resource/mgw2.021/?sp=201)

After the Jacobins, a new organization in Italy was formed containing Weishaupt's inner circle called the **Carbonari**. The highest level of the Carbonari was the "Alta Vendita." In 1818 they issued their mission statement which proclaimed,

Our final aim is that of Voltaire and the French Revolution, the destruction forever of Catholicism and even of the Christian idea, which if left standing on the ruins of Rome would be the resuscitation of Christianity later on. The work which we have undertaken is not the work of a day, nor of a month, nor of a year, it may last many years, a century perhaps, but in our ranks the soldier dies and the fight continues. (Grand Orient Freemasonry Unmasked, by Msgr. George F. Dillon, D.D., 1885, pg. 89-90)

Moving forward in history, toward the middle and latter half of the 1800s, we see the emergence of many new "-isms" all with the same goal of world power. These include Communism, Socialism, Nihilism, Anarchism and Syndicalism (taking power through the labor movement). All of these ideologies are direct descendants and useful means to an end employed by the Illuminati.

Be observant that these words have been redefined over the years in some cases. For example, anarchism is now often connected to freedom, but historically it has been used as a temporary transition from a previous system into a new system. In 1917, Communism became the first of the *-isms* to seize control of a physical base of operations. Communism very rapidly rose to such a pre-eminent position within the Conspiracy that today, it is known as the Communist Conspiracy. But to better understand the truth of that time, you must be aware that Communism is only a tool of the total Conspiracy, though directly connected to the Illuminists as admitted by Vladimir Lenin in a speech he gave May 28, 1918 *(see: Le Bolchevisme et le Jacobinisme. Paris, Librairie du Parti Socialiste et de l'Humanité, 1920)*.

Communism is merely a means for world rule by a group of brilliant criminals who have no loyalty to any economic, political, or social ideology. The Illuminists only loyalty is to themselves and their own structure.

There are some who wish to debate whether the Illuminati exists today. The group has necessarily and cleverly changed its bases of operation and its name over the years, in order to remain secret. The current name of the group really does not matter. What does matter is the presence today of a tightly knit organization that is using the tactics and having the same goal as the Illuminati. It is interesting, though certainly not conclusive, to note the adoption of May First, the date of the founding of the Illuminati in 1776, as the international holiday for Communists and Socialists the world over.

Some argue that, "If this Conspiracy exists, then it is reasonable to expect that someone, at some time, would defect from it and tell the world about it."

Those that make such remarks have no understanding of the covenant nature of the conspiracy to protect one another and destroy those that would defect against their goals; but withstanding those charges, there have been a divulging of secrets from the inside through defectors of various types at various levels.

One example is Dr. Carroll Quigley who, in 1966, wrote a lengthy book entitled *Tragedy and Hope*. Dr. Quigley was a professor of history who spent most of his years at Harvard and Princeton, and in later years at Georgetown University in Washington, DC. *Tragedy and Hope* is a history of this grand conspiracy, as he calls it. In this book, Dr. Quigley tells us of a "secret network" operating both here and in Europe to control the world. He details the role played by the Rothschilds and other banking families, the part played by the Council on Foreign Relations and its English equivalent, and the participation in this network of Edward Mandell House, the Dulles brothers, Walter Lippmann, and many others.

Finding admissions from modern day "Gadiantons" isn't very hard either. One such Gadianton said of himself and his associates,

> *Some even believe we are part of a secret cabal working against the best interests of the United States, characterizing my family and me as 'internationalists' and of conspiring with others around the world to build a more integrated global political and economic structure - one world, if you will. If that's the charge, I stand guilty, and I am proud of it.* (David Rockefeller, "Memoirs" page 405)

To help us understand who all of the players were and what they were working on in our day, in General Conference of April 1972, Ezra Taft Benson said,

> *There is no conspiracy theory in the Book of Mormon --it is a conspiracy fact. And along those lines, I would highly recommend to you the book NONE DARE CALL IT CONSPIRACY by Gary Allen.*

As author Gary Allen documents in his book, "None Dare Call It Conspiracy," this is not a

Republican vs. Democrat issue. There are wolves in sheep's clothing on both sides that, as Moroni explained, want to "overthrow the freedom of all lands, nations, and countries." Understanding that the goal of these modern Gadianton Robbers is to fill the "judgment seats" (fill all positions of government in our day) also helps us to understand who these people are as well as who they are not.

"None Dare Call It Conspiracy" also documents the efforts of the Council on Foreign Relations (CFR) as a group whose aim it is to fulfil the agenda that David Rockefeller admitted to in his own autobiography of "conspiring" to work "against the best interests of the United States." This organization has both Republicans and Democrats in government, media, and academia to promote their agenda.

In addition to "None Dare Call It Conspiracy," many have warned about the aims of the (CFR) making it unpopular (in many circles) to be associated with the organization. In fact, former Utah Governor Huntsman resigned from his membership because of this growing unpopularity. Others, though, just keep it a secret. Former Vice President of the United States, Dick Cheney, laughed about it saying,

It's great to be back at the Council on Foreign Relations... I've been a member for a long time and was actually director for some period of time. I never mentioned that when I was campaigning for election back home in Wyoming [audience laughs]. (Speech given at the CFR, 15 February 2002)

Hillary Clinton wasn't so shy about her association with the CFR when she admitted in July 2009,

I am delighted to be here in these new headquarters. I have been often to, I guess, the 'mother ship' in New York City, but it's good to have an outpost of the Council right here down the street from the State Department. We get a lot of advice from the Council, so this will mean I won't have as far to go to be told what we should be doing. (Speech given at the opening of the Washington DC branch of the Council on Foreign Relations)

Despite their ego-boosting low-profile admissions, Gadiantons fear true widespread exposure above all else, which is why they spend so much effort maligning those exposing the conspiracy and also why they spread false-conspiracies to confuse the public. Widespread exposure is an important piece of removing their power and fulfilling what Benson spoke about in 1961 when he said,

The Lord has declared that before the second coming of Christ it will be necessary to "destroy

With this brief overview of the international Conspiracy, this book will begin to document how it has worked its way into influencing and implanting the agenda on the people of Utah. We will reference more of the international conspiracy as we discuss its influence in Utah.

Important thoughts: Why would any person join a Secret Combination?

One of the natural results of studying secret combinations with sincerity, is learning about people, names, and organizations. It becomes real when you start to know who is involved. At first you may learn about David Rockefeller or Henry Kissinger and how they flaunt their power and involvement at a global level with no shame. But as the topic gets more localized, the names start to become people you may have met in political action, the business field, or perhaps they are influential people who you've run into in your own city. Maybe you know someone personally who has worked closely with a local power player that you now know is involved in building the new world order. With personal interactions, emotion, and genuine conversations muddying the water, this is much more difficult for the average "good person" to process.

It's important not to jump to conclusions and blame everyone who does something you don't like, but it's also important to be intellectually honest when the actions someone takes are very clearly aligned with a known agenda. We must have a healthy understanding that we are not privy to every personal circumstance of, nor the judge of, an individual's soul-- that is for Jesus Christ. But we are required to stand for and defend freedom when it is threatened, wherever that may come from, with reason, facts, and principles behind our words of warning.

So why would hundreds of people, who are just living their lives like normal people, one day, become caught up in a secret combination?

Ezra Taft Benson answers this very plainly, that "Pride results in secret combinations which are built up to get power, gain and glory of the world." As soon as people decide they're better than others, they deserve more than someone else, or they're clearly smarter and therefore superior to other people, the devil can potentially justify them taking actions in secret to satisfy what they want in the name of their pride. This situation officially is defined as a secret combination when the actions taken become criminal, meaning they violate the life, liberty, or property of someone else in any way. This can happen anywhere, and it is why Benson's talks on pride are some of the most important for the world today.

Benson's teachings on pride are some of the most quoted LDS teachings outside of the LDS church. Even the most well-meaning people in the most well-meaning organization can quickly start creating an inner circle to accomplish separate goals when they think they have a superior justification. That inner circle then justifies keeping secrets and organizations begin to crumble from the inside out—unless the cycle is stopped.

You don't have to be part of the big global conspiracy, to get caught up in the principle of a secret combination. However, the grand Satanic conspiracy can recruit new members by testing their pride and slowly introducing them into their circles.

Imagine wanting to make a difference in the world so you run for office with hopes to "fix the system," but then you lose an election to someone who didn't even try. You swore you did everything right and you thought you had it in the bag. Frustrated, you are then approached by a really nice guy who says, "you know, if you just joined this club, the next time you run for office you'll be guaranteed to win". It sure might boost your ego to know you've got powerful friends, right? You might think that you can join up and then make a difference after you have the power they give you? This scenario is far more common than most people think.

You can probably even maintain your morals for quite a while as you climb the ranks before you ever have to do anything truly "evil." Or maybe you never have to do anything "evil," you just have to be willing to always use your influence to speak against candidates they don't like while you enjoy your own power and influence. They may know you'll never compromise on anything big, but since you're a trusted friend, you'll get special government endorsed deals for your business that you rely on for your newfound wealth and power, and the only thing asked in return is that once a year the insiders club requires your successful and influential company to endorse and fund campaigns, whether you agree with the candidates or not.

Once again, this scenario is far more common than most people think.

Let us always remain humble and always know that we can accomplish nothing in our lives without God who gives us breath and life every second that we live. Let us do good with God's power and the resources and influence that we obtain through our honest labors in the bodies God gave us. Let us always consider correct principles in the details of our lives.

Chapter I
How We Got Here

The founder of Defending Utah, along with key volunteers, brainstormed this several years ago. In 2012 and 2013 we hypothesized,

> *This is a global conspiracy, and this conspiracy is ultimately a battle between Christ and Satan. And if that's really what this comes down to, then wouldn't it make sense that Satan would be following the same patterns? If they're doing horrible things in New York and California (like the exposed Bohemian grove rituals and Skull and Bones rituals), wouldn't it make sense that they're doing those things here if they wanted to oppose the LDS culture and teachings that are so strongly rooted here which preach against their agenda?*

With that hypothesis, we were able to start from the foundation of our understanding of the global conspiracy and expand from there. We began asking how the communist United Nations is implementing its program here in Utah at the local level, despite the teachings of the leaders of the past. We're supposed to be "conservative." How is this happening? How are all these different programs of the conspiracy being implemented in the state of Utah?

Defending Utah doesn't just talk about the principles of liberty and the principles of the constitution and limited government, we help you understand "why aren't we obeying the constitution anymore?" and understand that it isn't happening by accident. We don't believe in the "accidental theory of history"; we believe in the fact that history is replete with conspiracy.

Sometimes when you bring up the idea that we are facing conspiracy, it can make people feel overwhelmed and hopeless. In reality, we take the opposite approach because the things that we're facing are more like fires. We have high taxes, attacks on property rights, attacks on the unborn, attacks on the family…attack after attack after attack. If these weren't happening on purpose, and these were all "spontaneous fires" combusting all by themselves… if these were all things that we've got to focus on like a "whack-a-mole" game trying to shut down each fire… and they're all going to keep popping up with no end... that's what would be impossible to deal with. However, we understand that these fires are not happening by accident, that what we're facing is an arsonist starting fires on purpose. When we understand this analogy, we can be more effective in our efforts to preserve liberty and "destroy the secret combinations" in preparation for a future world where people live free under a righteous rule of law, which we'll get into.

When we talk about the grand conspiracy against mankind, before we can start to understand what's really going on, we must overcome a crippling habit: Too often we are tempted to reject the truths that we should otherwise learn because we're too focused on <u>who</u> is right as opposed to <u>what</u> is right. Truth must be valued above our favorite personalities. As Ezra Taft Benson described:

> *Pride does not look up to God and care about what is right. It looks sideways to man and argues who is right.*
> (Ezra Taft Benson, 1986, April Conference Report)

> *Pride is concerned with who is right. Humility is concerned with what is right.*
> (ETB Quote often paraphrased as such)

Today, we want to encourage all of us to do better in focusing on what's right instead of who's right. We're focusing on principles. The better we understand principles the easier it is to identify the wolves in sheep's clothing.

To those with a background in history and an understanding of the conspiracy in general, we want to give you some background on how the conspiracy came to Utah. To do that, we must explore the history of how the LDS saints came here.

Consider the pioneers, before they came to Utah, who wanted to live according to the principles of the Constitution. They lived in the united States where the Constitution should reign supreme. Unfortunately, because the federal government had apostatized from the constitution, persecuted them without just cause, and carried out violent attacks on their own citizens, the saints had to flee the united States. It can appear contradictory to say you must leave America to live according to the US Constitution, but when the government violated the constitution time and time again, they were forced to do exactly that to uphold the principles of the Constitution.

After the death of the Prophet Joseph Smith, the conspiracy was doing all it could to divide the saints and keep as many of them from remaining united under Brigham Young. James Strang and John C. Bennett were key players in this part of the conspiracy.

Bennett was an influential member of the Church due to his help in obtaining the charter from the state legislature for the city of Nauvoo.

However, just two years after joining the Church, Bennett was excommunicated for adultery, homosexual relations, and unauthorized plural marriages *(Samuel Taylor Papers, handwritten notes on typed page of rough draft of Nightfall at Nauvoo, unnumbered first page of Chapter VII, "Every Species of Abomination," Taylor Family Papers).* It also came out that Bennett was also an abortionist.

Two years later in April of 1844, James Strang joins the Church two months before Joseph Smith is assassinated/martyred while Strang is on a mission in Wisconsin *("Junius & Joseph" - Wicks & Foster, Utah State University Press, 2005).*

Strang and Bennett worked together to gather their own followings which undermined Brigham Young after he had been approved as Smith's rightful and legal successor.

It's certainly an interesting piece of history to note that these two formed an organization which they called the Halcyon Order of the Illuminati *(James Jesse Strang collection, 1846, WA MSS 447, box 2, Archives at Yale; "The Saintly Scoundrel" Andrew Smith, University of Illinois Press, pg. 150).*

These Illuminists were the originators of claims that Brigham Young invented doctrines that today the mainstream LDS church attributes to Joseph Smith. In addition to denying these teachings of

Joseph Smith, these Illuminists rejected Joseph Smith's translation of the Egyptian papyrus found in the Book of Abraham as well as Joseph Smith's endowment as restored while the saints were in Nauvoo.

Understanding this early Illuminati influence will help us overcome their lies about religion, freedom and history.

Alexis de Tocqueville's words were poignant when he explained what made American's so unique and capable of liberty. He attributed it to the fact that,

> *Every citizen is taught, the doctrines and the evidences of his religion, the history of his country, and the leading features of its Constitution.*

> *...it is extremely rare to find a man imperfectly acquainted with all these things, and a person wholly ignorant of them is a sort of phenomenon.*
> (Democracy in America, pg. 289)

Remaining ignorant of our history and the doctrines of our religion, allows these Satanists to change our history and destroy who we are. The Satanic conspiracy has not stopped its attempts to get the saints of God to reject these eternal truths and malign those that perpetuate them. It is interesting that in many growing circles of self-professed saints, especially among "academics", it is popular to be <u>extra</u> critical of Brigham Young and Ezra Taft Benson? Despite their human imperfections, they were arguably the strongest defenders of the principles of freedom in LDS history. This should be very revealing of the spirit directing these criticisms.

Eventually things began to calm down among the saints, and the remaining members of the Quorum of the Twelve, under the direction of the Council of Fifty, led the saints out of the united States in 1846.

The saints migrated west and formed an independent nation called Deseret. It was an independent nation with its own money, laws, culture, and society. But that didn't last very long. Less than two short years later, the conspiracy, using its usurped powers in the united States, sought to subjugate this independent nation. The future plans of the New World Order (the future world-communist/illuminist-controlled government) demanded that no nation/kingdom become independent of the planned global tyranny. Though the LDS saints claimed this territory as their own nation without any opposition from Mexico, the united States made its own counter-claim against Deseret. Despite how the people of Deseret assisted the united States during the Mexican-American war, the united States used the end of the war to enter into what was called the treaty of Guadalupe Hidalgo where they claimed Deseret as their own. The territory/nation became a disputed area with this claim from the united States, even though the loyalty of the people was to Deseret the nation.

To protect the LDS church's interests, the church created its own political party. This is a scan of "People's party" candidates in 1876. These days, Utah is accustomed to a culture where the church is

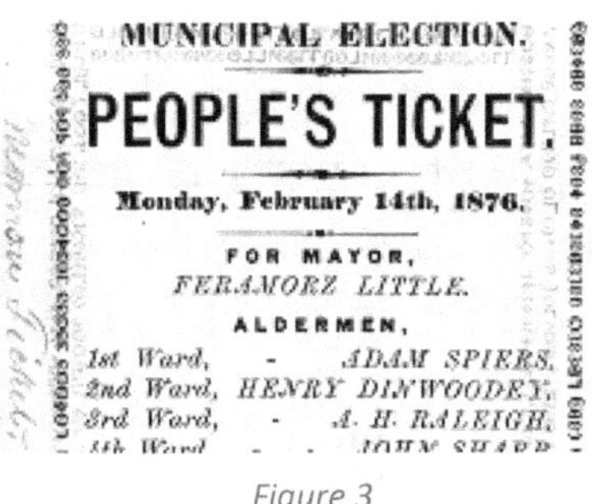

Figure 3

politically neutral. It seems strange to us that the church would have its own political party, but at this period in history it was a very normal practice. In fact, it seemed very necessary in the fight for maintaining liberty.

At the time, there was a lot of anti-Mormon sentiment being sent to Washington DC. In response, the united States sent Johnson's army to quell the so-called "Mormon rebellion." Johnson's army came to Deseret with the backing of the Orwellian-named federal "Utah Peace Commission". During this time, James Buchanan was the president of the united States, and as a part of the "peace commission," they deposed Brigham Young as the duly elected governor and told the people of Utah they were no longer allowed to choose their own leaders. In essence, they were told that, "the all-powerful all-knowing people in the federal government are going to send you a governor from a different state to make sure you don't get out of line."

From that time until Utah became a state, twelve different governors imposed on the territory by the federal government. In fact, one territorial governor who was known to be staunchly anti-Mormon (Eli Murray), removed nearly two hundred elected Mormons office. One tyrant unilaterally removed two hundred elected officials to be replaced by those loyal to him. (Utah: Struggle for Statehood, University of Utah Press & KUED, 2006, Disc 3 19:05)

These events led us to John Taylor and the First Presidency issuing a statement published in the Deseret news on 13 April 1886, saying,

> *The scenes which we are now witnessing in this territory are the results of a deep laid and carefully planned conspiracy, which has been in the process of formation for years. Its originators knew the elements they had to deal with, and by cunning contrivance they have affected a*

wonderful [Secret] combination. Religious and irreligious, ministers in sacerdotal robes and atheistic scoffers, businessmen of integrity and blacklegs, temperance men and drunkards, men of strict morality and pimps and harlots, are crowded together on the platform they have constructed, and they find no inconvenience from each other's companionship. Each is made to believe that it is to his direct interest to combine to destroy 'Mormonism'.

They were not afraid to use that word: "Conspiracy." They recognized it for what it is. Taylor said that the people who were involved in the conspiracy were the rich, the poor, the moral, the immoral, the religious, the irreligious, etc. All these people from different backgrounds were unified to destroy the local culture - all unified as "useful idiots" with their own independent motives, on behalf of somebody else's grand plan who is orchestrating it all.

At this point, we now find Utah with two cultures. On one side, were the saints who preached the constitution, individual liberty, and natural law. They went west to the mountains to live according to these principles. On the other side, you have a nation that has abandoned the things that it was founded upon (life, liberty and property, the Constitution, etc.), and this conspiracy is trying to merge these two cultures in an effort to "destroy 'Mormonism'." The conspirators are essentially saying to Deseret/Utah, "you can't leave us. You will merge with the world at all costs!" Again, keep in context the Illuminati's future plan for a New World Order that we now see plainly before us in the year 2022. All around the world, the battle for local power has been playing out for hundreds of years with their long-term goal in mind.

The question then is, how do you forcefully integrate two, diametrically opposed cultures?

You've probably heard it by different names but Karl Marx, in the Communist Manifesto, explains the process:

> *In the beginning this cannot be affected except by means of **despotic inroads** by means of measures therefore which appear economically insufficient and untenable but which in the course of the movement outstrip themselves and necessitate further inroads **upon the old social order**.*

When you break it down, Marx is talking about the "boiling the frog" approach. If you throw a live frog into a pot of boiling water, he will immediately jump out. But if you slowly turn up the heat, you will be able to boil the frog without any opposition. Marx says these things are done in "insufficient" and "untenable" ways, meaning each change is "not a big deal." It's so small that if you don't want to go along with it, you're made to look like the unreasonable one; you're the jerk for not being willing to compromise with other people. However, the conspiracy recognizes that each of those small changes has, within that change, the necessity for the next change and then for the next and for the next until, one degree at a time, you're a completely different people than you were in the beginning.

In thinking about how this works, you may recognize the "Hegelian Dialectic" of:
problem → reaction → solution, or
thesis → antithesis → synthesis, or
"the Overton window."

There are a few slightly different variations of this strategy. This strategy is a neutral tool, perhaps even a "natural law" that can be used for good or evil depending on who holds the tool.

Chapter II
The Conspiracy to Change the Culture

We now see that there is a conspiracy to get the pioneer-era saints to merge culturally back into the united States that has now abandoned the principles of the founding fathers. This conspiracy has a playbook on how to accomplish this goal. They have clearly targeted three different parts of the culture to accomplish their goals with the people of Deseret/Utah. What are the parts of the culture that the saints were building?

1. Economic Independence - independence as a nation.
2. Political Independence - adhering to principles of natural law and the Constitution & building the Kingdom of God.
3. Educational Independence – Parents, or those of the same beliefs, should oversee the education of children.

We must analyze each one of these aspects of culture, showing what the saints were trying to build and how the conspiracy was working to get them to abandon them.

Economic Independence

Know ye not that the friendship of the world is enmity with God? Whosoever therefore will be a friend of the world is the enemy of God. (James 4:4, KJV)

The ancient followers of Christ were separate from the Romans. To avoid being co-opted by them, they had to know how to provide for their own well-being, independent of the Empire.

Mormon theology has taught this same principle again in modern times, and it is simply a natural law that we can observe in nature. If you're dependent on another entity for your survival, that other entity can have control over you, telling you what to do or what not to do to obtain compliance through threatening to withhold basic necessities. It's why, as a culture, free-people must reject dependence on government handouts.

In 2 Nephi 26:31 we learn that,

> *But the laborer in Zion shall labor for Zion; for if they labor for money they shall perish.*

The Lord told the early saints,

> *[T]he decree hath gone forth from the Father that they shall be gathered in unto one place upon the face of this land, to prepare their hearts and be prepared in all things against the day when*

tribulation and desolation are sent forth upon the wicked. (Doctrine and Covenants 29:8)

Then again,

[T]he time has come when the voice of the Lord is unto you: Go ye out of Babylon; gather ye out from among the nations, from the four winds, from one end of heaven to the other. (Doctrine and Covenants 133:7)

Joseph Smith taught this principle when he said,

The Lord says that we shall never do another day's work nor spend another dollar to build up a gentile city or nation. (Journal of Discourses 11:295)

Orson Pratt echoed this sentiment when he taught,

Ever since the settlement of this Territory I have felt how much better it would be if this people would unite together and appoint their merchants to go and buy their goods and bring them here and sell them at a reasonable profit to the rest of the community, and never trade here to the amount of one dime with those who are outside of us. (Journal of Discourses 12:305)

Leaders taught as revealed doctrine that the saints were not supposed to do another day's work nor spend another dollar building up "Babylon" so that they could be independent and cease aiding those that would use their money against them.

Brigham Young explained,

> *They want the Mormons to build cities for them
> to possess and this we shall do no more for them.*
> (Journal of Discourses 11:278)

This had become a pattern of suffering for the early saints. First, building up Missouri and then being driven out. Next, building up Illinois, and then being driven out. And finally, fleeing to Utah and now seeing the same pattern unfold.

Brigham Young continues,

> *If we build cities, we mean to possess them.* (Ibid.)

It would be a contradiction for us to spend our time and resources to strengthen a movement that was working to take what we have built, but that is exactly what we have become and continue to support. Taking away resources that come from our labors that should be used to build an independent economy instead of the economy of a New World Order.

Apostle Daniel H. Wells taught,

> *Now all you that freight for the Gentiles, that go
> out on the road in the employ of the Gentiles
> driving stage, or trading and working at the beck
> of the Devil, to promote the Devil's kingdom; let
> me exhort you to turn about and not continue to*

mingle with the wicked. You had better never see a dime in the world.

Need I say a word against our brethren going and engaging themselves to do this when they so well understand that it is not the Mission of the Latter-day Saints to labor for anything but the upbuilding of the Church and Kingdom of God?

let them herd their own cattle, delve in the earth for themselves, gather their own straw, make their own mortar, build up their own cities, but let us raise our own cotton, indigo, tobacco, build up our own cities — even the cities of Zion for the honor and glory of God. (Journal of Discourses 9:301-302)

Shortly after, the first governor imposed on Deseret by the federal government came to speak to the state legislature. He said,

Many of the laws now on the statute book were passed under a condition of things [economic independence], which will soon cease to exist. You cannot reasonably anticipate a continuance of the partial isolation which has characterized your early history in this region... New relations between yourselves and the outer world must occur. I would, therefore, urge upon you that you appoint committees to prepare the code of laws, suited to the present and future requirements of this community. (Territorial

Governor Alfred Cumming, Communication to the Legislative Assembly of Utah Annexed to the Governor's Message, 10 December 1860)

In Utah government school history books and classes, they teach that early Utahns were begging to rejoin the union. This falsehood is clear, as we can see this was all done through machinations, blackmail and other threats of force and coercion. Why would the LDS leave an oppressive nation and then beg to rejoin it?

Kingdom of God

The second part of the culture of the early Utah saints was building the literal Kingdom of God and not submitting to unconstitutional government. The concept of the Kingdom of God was advanced into very practical ideas and concrete steps as recorded through Joseph Smith's revelation in the minutes of the Council of 50, published by the LDS church. Deseret was intended to be this Kingdom of God, that would eventually accept Jesus Christ's return to the earth. This separate nation was to be one of limited government, that would honor the same principles of the US Constitution, governed by the Council of 50 which must govern by making unanimous decisions. Appeal to the head or king could be made if the 50 were not able to reach a unanimous decision. A mixture of religions was required to participate on the council (it could not be all Mormons or Christ would not accept the council). There would be elements of a republic that would protect and hold sacred the individual freedoms of all within the borders of the Kingdom. It was anticipated that Jesus Christ would take the lead as King of the world, and everything else was preparatory to that day.

Consider that this political move stems from one of the most foundational beliefs that Joseph Smith wrote in the Articles of Faith: the fundamental belief of letting all people choose their own religion or non-religion; Free Agency. The saints believed the US Constitution to be nearly scripture, given to the world by Jesus Christ Himself. When they saw that even the united States who was governed by this document was failing to honor their rights, they sought to take the responsibility on themselves (See minutes of the Council of 50, and the Constitution of the Kingdom of God).

Jesus Christ made us free to choose everything, good or bad, for ourselves, and we absolutely must allow all people to live freely. This is the most important political difference between Christ's kingdom and the New World Order. In order for the saints to claim their rights, they had to create a country where they (and all others) would be afforded their rights, and so they had to create it themselves. While the political Kingdom of God has a theologically driven belief that Christ is King, it is absolutely founded on the idea that the principles of freedom are for everyone in the entire world without exception. It is not "church rule," it is civic rule where freedom is defended with religious fervor. The church itself was a different entity from the Kingdom of God.

Church president John Taylor famously said, "I defy the united States!" Now, today we think of this idea of civil disobedience being outside of our cultural norms here in Utah, but during these times, when the government was breaking the law (doing something unconstitutional), it was our job to defy the united States as an act of upholding the law that we held sacred.

> *We are today a kingdom of priests holding to a very great extent the holy priesthood; and it is essential that we submit to the laws of that priesthood and be governed by them in all of our actions.* (John Taylor, Journal of Discourses 21:358)

This attitude stemmed from the Biblical examples of God's earthly Kingdom being established and its prophesied establishment in the last days. The early saints read their scriptures and saw the Kingdom's establishment in the days of Adam, Enoch, Abraham, Moses, and others. The saints also read about the prophesied time in the Last Days when it would be established again.

When Daniel interpreted King Nebuchadnezzars dream, he saw,

> *And in the days of these kings shall the God of heaven set up a kingdom, which shall never be destroyed: and the kingdom shall not be left to other people, but it shall break in pieces and consume all these kingdoms, and it shall stand for ever. Forasmuch as thou sawest that the stone was cut out of the mountain without hands.* (Daniel 2:44-45, KJV)

John The Revelator also foresaw this event of the last days,

> *And there appeared a great wonder in heaven; a woman clothed with the sun, and the moon under her feet, and upon her head a crown of twelve stars: And she being with child cried, travailing in birth, and pained to be delivered. And she brought forth a man child, who was to rule all nations with a rod of iron…* (Revelation 12: 1-2, 5, KJV)

Though the saints were staunch defenders of the Constitution of the united States, they understood the Constitution itself wasn't the end game. Orson Pratt explained,

But with all its glory and greatness and perfection, it was only a steppingstone to a form of government infinitely greater and more perfect—a government founded upon Divine laws, with all its institutions, ordinances, and officers appointed by the God of heaven. (Journal of Discourses 7:215)

The topic of building the Kingdom of God was a regular topic from the pulpit with the phrase "The Kingdom of God or nothing!" being a common rallying cry, and they understood they weren't talking about building the Church when they said this. They repeatedly taught that the Church and the Kingdom of God were two separate institutions with two very different missions. Returning to the saint's time in Nauvoo,

Joseph Smith then explained that the two were distinct, as the church was not designed to "govern men in civil matters" and the kingdom was 'not designed to affect our salvation hereafter. (18 April 1844, Hancock Co., IL, Joseph Smith Papers, Administrative Records, Council of Fifty Minutes, 2016, pg. 108)

The Kingdom was an institution that governed men in civil matters, not ecclesiastical. Joseph then explained the Church's role and what the ancient prophet Daniel saw,

There is a distinction between the Church of God and kingdom of God... It is an entire, distinct and separate government. The church is a spiritual matter and a spiritual kingdom; but the kingdom which Daniel saw was not a spiritual kingdom, but was designed to be got up for the safety and salvation of the saints by protecting them in their religious rights and worship. (Ibid., p. 128)

George Q. Cannon continued the teachings of Joseph Smith when he taught,

We have been taught from the beginning this important principle, that the church of God is distinct from the kingdom of God. In the midst of all of us who understand this matter there is a clear distinction between the church in its ecclesiastical capacity and that which may be termed the government of God in its political capacity. (Juvenile Instructor 31:140)

...the kingdom of God ... is to become a political power, known and recognized by the powers of the earth; and you, my brethren, may have to be sent forth to represent that power as its accredited agents. (Millennial Star, 24:103)

This was a political organization for directing the temporal affairs of the people. As John Taylor clearly pointed out,

God has established His Church, and we sometimes say His kingdom. What do we mean by the Kingdom of God?... There is the Church of God and the Kingdom of God. The Church of course, refers more particularly to spiritual things, and the kingdom to temporal rule and government and management and to temporal affairs. (Journal of Discourses, Volume 20:166)

The saints were being driven from State to State, having their God-given rights regularly trampled upon, their homes being destroyed and their women and children being brutally raped while supposedly under the protection of the government, and when they reached out to government officials to claim their constitutionally protected right of redress, the best response they could get was "your cause is just, but I can do nothing for you" *(President Martin Van Buren, 1839).* Joseph was seeking for answers from the Lord on how to act with the government turning its back on the Constitution and he,

[O]rganized into a special counsel to take into consideration... the best policy for this people to adopt to obtain their rights from the nation and secure protection for themselves and children; and to secure a resting place in the mountains, or some uninhibited region, where we can enjoy the liberty of conscience guaranteed to us by the

However, the Kingdom of God is not just for the protection of one group, but for the protecting of the liberty of all. George Q. Cannon explained,

> *The Kingdom of God when established will not be for the protection of [one church] alone, but for the protection of all men, whatever their religious views or opinions may be. Under its rule, no one will be permitted to overstep the proper bounds or to interfere with the rights of others.* (Journal of Discourses, 6:342)

Brigham Young, being a staunch supporter of individual liberty, went further saying,

> *[The Kingdom of God] will throw their protecting arms around the whole human family, protecting them in their rights. If they wish to worship a white dog, they will have the privilege, if they wish to worship the sun, they will have the privilege, if they wish to worship a man they will have the privilege, if they wish to worship the "unknown God" they will have the privilege. This kingdom will circumscribe them all and will issue laws and ordinances to protect them in their rights – every right that every people, sect and person can enjoy, and the full liberty that God has granted to them without molestation.* (Journal of Discourses, 7:382)

This Kingdom, designed to protect everyone's rights, was something they envisioned becoming a real political power. George Q. Cannon stated,

> *The kingdom of God… is to become a political power, known and recognized by the powers of the earth; and you, my brethren, may have to be sent forth to represent that power as its accredited agents.* (Millennial Star, 24:103)

Orson Pratt said that the Constitution of the united States was a stepping stone to the Kingdom of God, however, the two governments were not radically different from each other. Brigham Young states,

> *But few, if any, understand what a theocratic government is. In every sense of the word, it is a republican government, and differs but little in form from our National, State, and Territorial Governments; but its subjects will recognize the will and dictation of the Almighty.*
>
> *Even now the form of the Government of the United States differs but little from that of the kingdom of God.* (Journal of Discourses, 6:342 & 345)

Though they recognized and honored this fact, the saints realized the Kingdom of God had to be established outside the confines of the united States, especially since it had abandoned the Constitution that was meant to bind it down to protecting the rights of the people. A society meant to protect the rights of the people, cannot be established in the midst of a government and people controlled by a conspiracy dedicated to the opposite program.

> *You all know and have doubtless felt for years the necessity of a removal provided the government should not be sufficiently protective to allow us to worship God according to the dictates of our own consciences, and of the omnipotent voice of eternal truth. Two cannot walk together except they be agreed.* (Brigham Young, B.H. Roberts's Edition: History of the Church, 2: 478-479)

The saints were finally able to separate themselves and migrated west to build the Kingdom prophesied by prophets of old.

Ordained a "King and a Priest" by Joseph Smith at the "Last charge" in the spring of 1844, Brigham Young was now at the head of this Kingdom. *((Times and Seasons, September 15, 1844, 651; James R. Clark, comp., Messages of the First Presidency of The Church of Jesus Christ of Latter-day Saints (Salt Lake City: Bookcraft, 1966), 3:134))*

To help the saints understand what this meant, Brigham consistently instilled in them the understanding needed to build this Kingdom. Helping build this understanding was his laser like focus.

My face is set like a flint for this. I never expect to cease calculating, planning, and executing, until this people can organize from the native elements, everything they wish for life, for decoration, and for beauty, in their existence, upon this earth, preparatory to their being laid away in the silent grave, as the fathers and mothers of a free and independent nation. These are also the feelings of this great people, of every man and woman who has the cause of Zion at heart. (10 April 1853, SLC Tabernacle Afternoon conference. Millennial Star 16:673-675)

In the middle of the Deseret invasion by the united States government, Brigham Young said,

The time must come when there will be a separation between this kingdom and the kingdoms of this world, even in every point of view. The time must come when this kingdom must be free and independent from all other kingdoms. Are you prepared to have the thread cut to-day? (Journal of Discourses 5:96-100)

Brigham knew that the Kingdom would not be established quickly, but prophesied the day would come:

We have a nation here in the mountains that will be a kingdom by-and-by and be governed by pure laws and principles. What do you call yourselves? some may ask. Here are the people

that constitute the kingdom of God. It may be some time before that kingdom is fully developed, but the time will come when the kingdom of God will reign free and independent. (Journal of Discourses 5:327-33)

With the united States' ongoing war against the saints and the Kingdom of God, Brigham Young declared,

that the thread was cut between us and the U.S. and that the Almighty recognized us as a free and independent people and that no officer appointed by government will come and rule over us from this time forth. (Manuscript Addresses of Brigham Young 3:71)

The nationhood of the Kingdom of God was reflected in the music of the day with songs proclaiming,

o Zion! Dear Zion! Land of the free… thy land shall be freedoms abode. (O Ye Mountains High, words written by Charles W. Penrose, put to music by H.S. Thompson, 1852)

High on the mountain top a banner is unfurled. Ye nations, now look up; it waves to all the world… (High on the Mountain Top, originally titled "DESERET", written by Joel H. Johnson, 1850)

Since the Federal Government had invaded Deseret, deposed its duly elected governor, and continued to trample on the rights of the people, the saints, acting in defense of the principles of the Constitution, and in accordance with their efforts to build the literal Kingdom of God, tried to act as if they had not been disenfranchised. In fact, John W. Taylor, the son of Church president John Taylor, explained that even though we have these governors imposed on us by the federal government, "the legislature took no action without approval of the church president" (John Taylor Papers, Taylor Trust Publishing, 1985, 2: 394). The people of Utah were still, culturally speaking, saying 'no, the head of the Kingdom of God is really the head of this government.' John Taylor explained this principle again when he says,

> *What do we mean by "the kingdom of God?" There is the church of god and the kingdom of God. The church refers to more spiritual things and the kingdom to temporal rule and government.* (Journal of Discourses, 20:166)

As a people, we understood, at this point in time, that the Kingdom of God and the Church of God were two separate organizations with two very separate goals and programs.

The Satanic Conspiracy wanted to do all it could to stop the progress of the Kingdom. But how do they do it without ruling over the people of Utah like a common European dictator, thus triggering the sympathies of the people not yet seeing the Mormons as a threat? It was evident to many people in this region of the continent that the Mormons just wanted to be left alone, as evidenced by their leaving the united States to an undesirable plot of desert land.

The conspiracy decided to use the "Victorian morals" of the day to mask their real motives and attack what the First Presidency of the Church said in their appeal for amnesty "was a necessity to man's highest exaltation in the life to come" (19 December 1891, First Presidency Petition for Amnesty, Contributor 13:197; Smoot Investigation Vol 1, p. 18). That "necessity" was, as the same statement called, "polygamy, or celestial marriage as commanded by God through Joseph Smith" (Ibid.). Any discussion about this marriage practice is not the subject of this book, but we must make it clear that the historical record shows that it was unjustly used as the excuse for this conspiracy to destroy the political independence of Deseret, and thus the intended bastion of freedom for the world which the saints hoped for.

Using these "Victorian morals" to crush this idea of the Kingdom of God and to force the Latter-day Saints to again merge into that national system, the conspiracy used their agents in congress to pass a series of anti-polygamy legislation that only applied to the Latter-day Saints.

One of the laws passed in 1882, the Edmonds Act, prohibited believing members of the Church from voting, holding office, or serving on a jury regardless of whether an individual was engaged in plural marriage or not. Despite this initial act, the saints continued to build the Kingdom of God by nullifying (ignoring) the illegal acts of Congress for a few years. In hopes of breaking the Saints, the Conspiracy then gets Congress to pass the Edmonds-Tucker Act in 1887. This bill disincorporated the church, dissolving it as a legal entity. This was the beginning of the movement for government permission (license) to get married (section 9), it banned religious books in schools (section 25), it required anti-polygamy oaths to the government (section 24). This act also confiscated all of the church's property (section 13, 16 & 17). This was a direct attack on the Church.

Following the Edmonds-Tucker Act, we fast forward to 1889/1890 and the Cullom-Struble Bill. This bill went a step further than the Edmonds-Tucker Act and declared that it didn't matter what you believed, nor what you practiced, just simply being a member of the Church of Jesus Christ of Latter-day Saints meant you were stripped of all rights of citizenship. You could not own property, you could not vote, you could not serve on a jury. The effect of this was that if you were accused of a crime, everybody on your jury could be someone that wanted to put you, as a Latter-day Saint, in prison. No LDS would be allowed a jury of their peers, as the constitution guaranteed. This applied not just to Latter-day Saints in Utah, but anywhere in the Union.

Frank Cannon represented Utah in Congress at this time and was the son of George Q. Cannon of the First Presidency of the Church of Jesus Christ of Latter-day Saints. Frank enlisted his father's help along with other leading members of the Church and friendly nonmembers to try and kill this bill.

This piece of legislation had a lot of support and had a real chance of passage, passing its first committee vote on April 29th 1890.

The author of the bill, Protestant attorney, future mayor of Salt Lake City and associate justice of the Supreme Court of Utah, Robert Newton Baskin, said he wrote the bill to, "Take away the political power" of "the Priesthood" *(Robert Newton Baskin, Reminiscences of Early Utah, 1914, p. 184)*.

As his legislation progressed, Baskin spoke with Senator Cullom, the bill's sponsor, who told him that he,

[H]ad been assured by a delegation of prominent Mormons, that if further action on the bill was delayed for a reasonable time, the practice of polygamy would be prohibited by the Mormon church. (Robert Newton Baskin, Reminiscences of Early Utah, 1914, p.184)

Baskin said that Representative Struble had received the same information.

In further efforts to kill the bill, Frank Cannon told members of the Senate that the Church "was about to make a concession concerning… polygamy." But Cannon wanted them to keep this information in confidence, "since to make public the news of such a concession, in advance, would be to prevent the Church from authorizing it." *(Frank J. Cannon and Knapp, Brigham Young, pg. 93)*

Frank Cannon testified before the Senate Committee on Territories that the bill would punish a "class of people who have obeyed the laws, and who swear they will not aid or abet anybody else". He also said that it would cause the youth and young adults in the Church to disavow the practice of plural marriage stating that,

They do disavow it [plural marriage] two or three times a year, usually. Every time they take this oath [provided by the Edmunds-Tucker Act] they disavow it (Political Deliverance, Edward Lyman,

University of Illinois Press 1986, pg 145. See also Hearings Before the Senate Committee on Territories in Relation to the Exercise of the Elective Franchise in the Territory of Utah, 51st Cong., 1st Session, microfilm copy, Lee Library, Brigham Young University, Provo, Utah).

To which we read the following conversation between Cannon and Senator Payne:

> *Senator Payne: Would they have the power to amend the creed of the church?*
>
> *Mr. Cannon: They Have not the Power.*
>
> *Senator Payne: If they had the power would they do it?*
>
> *Mr. Cannon: I think so.* (Ibid.)

Following the hearings, Frank Cannon met with Secretary of State, James Blaine, who tells Frank Cannon:

> *Believe me, it's not possible for any people as weak in numbers as yours, to set themselves up as superior to the majesty of a nation like this. We may succeed, this time, in preventing your disfranchisement; but nothing permanent can be done until you get into line... You may tell your father for me-as I tell you, young man- you shall not be harmed, **this time** [emphasis added].* (Frank J. Cannon, Under the Prophet in Utah: the National Menace of a Political Priestcraft, The C.M Clark Publishing Co. Boston, Massachusetts 1911, page 90, emphasis added.)

Blaine essentially threatening, "We're going to keep going after you until you do what we say."

George Q. Cannon's response to this encounter was to tell Frank,

> *President Woodruff has been praying... He thinks he sees some light... You are authorized to say that something will be done.*

and Frank understood that to mean:

> *the Church was preparing to concede a recession from the doctrine of polygamy.* (Ibid., pg. 91)

Senator Cullom told the bill's author that,

> *he had been assured by a delegation of prominent Mormons, that if further action on the bill was delayed for a reasonable time, the practice of polygamy would be prohibited by the Mormon Church... the request for delay was granted, but with the express understanding that if polygamy was not prohibited within a reasonable time vigorous steps would be taken to procure the passage of the bill.* (Reminiscences of Early Utah, Robert Newton Baskin, Tribune-Reporter Printing Company 1914, pg.184)

The bill had been delayed, and on September 24th, 1890, Church President, Wilford Woodruff, issued what is known as "The Manifesto" as found in the Official Declaration 1 in the Doctrine and

Covenants, leading to the eventual ending of authorized plural marriages in the Church. According to several accounts, the manifesto was written by Apostle Charles W. Penrose, Frank Cannon, John White, and George Reynolds. *(Matthias F. Cowley, Minutes of the Quorum of the Twelve, 10 May 1911; Reed Smoot Hearings 2:52-53).*

Though the conspiracy used a lot of distraction to introduce such legislation, there was a hidden agenda behind these tactics. The author of the Cullom-Strumble Bill, Robert Newton Baskin, one of the least famous, yet most influential, people in Utah's history, explained the real reasoning behind his writing and lobbying for this bill saying,

> *The purpose of the bill was to wrest from the hands of the priesthood the political power which it had so long wrongfully usurped and shamefully abused.* (Robert Newton Baskin, Reminiscences of early Utah, 1914, page 184)

Going after the Kingdom of God was the goal of this conspiracy, as confirmed by one of the governors of Utah imposed on us in the 1880s, Eli Murray. In a report to Washington on the goings on here in Utah he said,

> *What [do I] care as to the belief of those who regard Joe Smith as a prophet? Those who believe*

so are entitled to their belief. Their right to that belief, [I] would defend, if necessary, but obedience to law is required, and the exercise of temporal power by ecclesiastical authority, in the least degree, will no longer be tolerated. (Governor Eli H. Murray, "The Crisis in Utah", North American review, April 1882 pg. 346)

The united States invaded sovereign territory, placing appointed bureaucrats, such as Eli Murray, to rule over the people and instead of following the first amendment which specifically protects, "the free exercise of religion," he wanted total and absolute obedience from his subjects. He went on to say,

If the Mormons continue to [promote liberty and the kingdom of God], the sword will be invoked to subdue them… Either the Church will have to surrender or the government will. (Governor Eli H. Murray, 10 January 1886, The John Taylor Papers, Samuel Taylor, 2:394)

There was no question in the minds of this conspiracy: they had to destroy the Kingdom of God. This was the line in the sand because this is a battle between Christ and Satan.

EDUCATION

We now discuss principle three: educational independence.

Mormons took education very seriously as a scriptural doctrine from the very beginning.

> *It was the will of the Lord, made known shortly after the organization of the Church, that steps should be taken to have the children of the members taught in schools conducted under the influence of those who had faith in the Gospel.* (Joseph Fielding Smith, Church History and Modern Revelation, 4 vols. [Salt Lake City: The Church of Jesus Christ of Latter-day Saints, 1946-1949], 2: 98 – 99.)

As early as June 1831, the Lord commanded W.W. Phelps to,

> *assist my servant Oliver Cowdery to do the work of printing, and of selecting and writing books for schools in this church, that little children also may receive instruction before me as is pleasing unto me.* D&C 55:4

Church schools were set up wherever members of the Church were gathered. After the pioneers had arrived in the Salt Lake Valley and established themselves there, they again organized Church schools for the education and instruction of the youth of Zion. Although these were "Church Schools", they were not fully funded by the Church any more than BYU is now.

Although there were attendance fees to help pay for full time teachers and other staff, President Brigham Young felt that education was so important that he paid,

> *the school fee of several children who (were) either orphans or sons and daughters of poor people.* (Journal of Discourses, vol. 18 p. 357)

During the 1870s and 1880s, there was again a great outcry from the outside world that the "Mormons" were getting too much power and influence. To help "combat" this, it was proposed that before becoming a state there must be an "establishment of free schools" which would "prohibit the teaching of denominational sentiments in them." *(Boston Watchman, impression of Sept. 5th, 1878)*

Additionally, during the 1870s and 1880s, Protestant missionary societies established ninety free schools in Utah, hoping to win Latter-day Saint children away from the faith of their parents through "education."

With the very natural inclination to want the "less costly" option, many Latter-day Saint families started to send their children to these "free" schools set up by the government, which were funded through taxpayer dollars, as well as those set up by other faiths. Others just stopped paying the school fees though their children continued to attend the Church schools. This added much financial pressure on the Church schools and, since the teachers received their pay through these attendance fees, many of them were forced to find other employment.

Throughout this crisis in education, Utah's leaders were constantly reinforcing their position and warning the Saints of what would happen if they rejected correct principles of education.

Two principles that they focused on were:

- Free schools by taxation are theft
- Only those with your same values should teach your children.

We will address these principles in order.

Theft

Brigham Young taught:

> *I am opposed to free education as much as I am opposed to taking away property from one man and giving it to another… Would I encourage free schools by taxation? No!* (Journal of Discourses, vol. 18 p. 357)

The main argument for funding education through taxation is to provide an opportunity for the poor, who would not otherwise be able to afford to pay for their education. The idea of rejecting forced charity is found in this part of Utah's history and consistently through the majority of the history of the LDS church.

Regarding forced charity through taxation, President Benson said,

> *Occasionally, we receive questions as to the propriety of Church members receiving government assistance instead of Church assistance. Let me restate what is a fundamental principle. Individuals, to the extent possible, should provide for their own needs. Where the individual is unable to care for himself, his family should assist. Where the family is not able to provide, the Church should render assistance, not the government. We accept the basic principle that "though the people support the*

government, the government should not support the people." (General Conference, April 1977)

Elder Boyd K Packer added,

If a member is unable to sustain himself, then he is to call upon his own family, and then upon the Church, in that order, and not upon the government at all. (General Conference, April 1978)

Expanding on this, President Benson says,

When you accept food stamps, you accept an unearned handout that other working people are paying for. You do not earn food stamps or welfare payments. Every individual who accepts an unearned government gratuity is just as morally culpable as the individual who takes a handout from taxpayers' money to pay his heat, electricity, or rent. There is no difference in principle between them… The price you pay for 'something for nothing' may be more than you can afford. Do not rationalize your acceptance of government gratuities by saying, 'I am a contributing taxpayer too.' By doing this you contribute to the problem which is leading this nation to financial insolvency. (A Vision and A Hope for the Youth of Zion, BYU speeches, 1977)

Here President Benson teaches that accepting government gratuities in any form is the same.

Why is it wrong to accept these government gratuities?

In D&C 121 we read,

> *Behold, there are many called, but few are chosen. And why are they not chosen?*
>
> *...That the rights of the priesthood are inseparably connected with the powers of heaven, and that the powers of heaven cannot be controlled nor handled only upon the principles of righteousness. That they may be conferred upon us, it is true; but when we undertake to cover our sins, or to gratify our pride, our vain ambition, or to exercise control or dominion or compulsion upon the souls of the children of men, in any degree of unrighteousness, behold, the heavens withdraw themselves; the Spirit of the Lord is grieved; and when it is withdrawn, Amen to the priesthood or the authority of that man.* (Vs 32, 36-37)

From "Many Are Called, But Few Are Chosen," recommended by Ezra Taft Benson in General Conference April 1972, it says,

> *Men may exercise unrighteous dominion upon one another through the agency of government in just as many ways as they can when acting outside its framework. The most common method, however, is by denying or interfering*

with the right to own and control property, one of the elements of freedom.

...applying the Golden Rule, put yourself in 'A's' shoes. He has already given all he desires to charity. Are you not violating his conscience when you compel him to give more? Would you enjoy having someone dictate how much you must give to your church, a hospital or college? Would not this be a plain case of theft? And if you pass a law and legalize the taking and the giving, have you really changed the essential nature of the act? Haven't you merely legalized stealing? (page 37)

Even if we feel comfortable contributing money towards something, no matter how noble the cause, we have no right to compel another to do the same. To force another to support a cause or institution is unrighteous dominion and theft.

This principle is fundamental to the foundation of our society. Ezra Taft Benson, explaining the source of government power said,

> *Keep in mind that the people who have created their government can give to that government only such powers as they themselves have. They cannot give that which they do not possess.*

> *In a primitive state, there is no doubt that each man would be justified in using force, if*

necessary, to defend himself against physical harm, against theft of the fruits of his labor, and against enslavement by another. (Conference Report, Oct. 1968, pp. 18-19)

Taught by Latter-day Saints

The Lord commissioned WW Phelps and Oliver Cowdery to help in selecting and writing curriculum for the teaching of young Latter-day Saints. Why select these seemingly unqualified men? Why not just follow the recommendations of the most learned professors? Wouldn't they be more qualified to prescribe the most suitable books?

When this argument is used in the discussion of educating Latter-day Saint children, this talk by President Benson seems relevant,

> *I would rather have my child exposed to smallpox, typhus fever, cholera, or other malignant and deadly diseases than to the degrading influence of a corrupt teacher. It is infinitely better to take chances with an ignorant, but pure-minded teacher than with the greatest philosopher who is impure.* (General Conference, October 1970)

The importance of having Latter-day Saint children taught by Latter-day Saints was made clear by President John Taylor when he said,

> *And then we want to study also the principles of education, and to get the very best teachers we can to teach our children; see that they are men and women who fear God and keep his commandments. We do not want men or women to teach the children of the Latter-day Saints who are not Latter-day Saints themselves. Hear it, you Elders of Israel?* (Journal of Discourses 20:179)

This exact phrase was quoted and taught again in General Conference of April 1958, and the principle continues to be taught today.

President Taylor also questioned the ability of parents to enter the Celestial Kingdom if they deprive their children of this blessing,

> *I am told in the revelations to bring up my children in the fear of God. Now we are engaged in building our temples that we may become united and linked together by eternal covenants that shall exist in all time and throughout eternity. And then when we have done all this go and deliberately turn our children over to whom? To men who do not believe the Gospel, to men who, according to your faith are never going to the celestial kingdom of God. And you will*

turn your children over to them. And you call yourselves Latter-day Saints, do you? I will suppose a case.

You expect to be saved in the celestial kingdom of God. Well, supposing your expectations are realized, which I sometimes doubt, and you look down, down somewhere in a terrestrial or telestial kingdom, as the case may be, and you see your children, the offspring that God had given you to train up in his fear, to honor him and keep his commandments. And supposing they could converse with you what would be their feelings toward you? It would be, Father, Mother, you are to blame for this. I would have been with you if you had not tampered with the principles of life and salvation in permitting me to be decoyed away by false teachers, who taught incorrect principles. And this is the result of it. But then I very much question men and women's getting into the Celestial kingdom of God who have no more knowledge about principles of life and salvation than to go and tamper with the sacred offspring, the principle of life which God entrusted to your care, to thus shuffle it off to imbibe the spirit of unbelief, which leads to destruction and death. (Journal of Discourses 20:107)

If we expect any institution to teach principles that would threaten its existence, we expect "what never was and never will be." Government schools cannot and will not teach what our nation was founded upon. It cannot and will not teach the values that will lead the next generation to be the leaders that are needed to build God's kingdom. If we want our children to have that knowledge, we cannot remain in a system that teaches the opposite principles.

What an individual or organization funds will reflect that individual's or organization's values. This should not be shocking to anyone. Education has been seen by friends and enemies alike as the way to shape the future. Soviet dictator and mass murderer, Joseph Stalin stated that,

> *Education is a weapon, whose effect depends on who holds it in his hands and at whom it is aimed.*

The "father" of modern government education, John Dewey, explained the concept further when he said,

> *If the public schools can keep children occupied from 7:00 or 7:30 in the morning, throughout the day, with sports after school, and homework in the evening, the parents will have less than an hour a day with their children, and the family's and Chris-tian church's influence over them could be broken in about a generation. (Donald N.*

Sills, "Crisis in Education–An American Enigma" 1994, p. 1)

This "weapon" to "break" the faith of the child was made clear by religionists as well. In a conference of the Presbyterian church, it was boasted that,

> *Our schools unsettle the faith of the children of Mormonism. These schools develop into Churches as a rule. They [the schools] are the entering wedge to split parental opposition through the children.* (1881 General Assembly of the Presbyterian Church)

Another religious body that used schooling as a way to break the faith of the children were the Episcopalians. Bishop Danial Tuttle bragged,

> *In Utah, especially, schools were the backbone of our missionary work. Adults were fanatics, and so far beyond the reach of our influence… But the plastic minds and wills of the young we could hope to win.* (Daniel Tuttle, Reminiscences of a Missionary Bishop. New York: Thomas Thitaker, 1906. p. 373)

This has been a useful tactic of the communists around the world. In Afghanistan, the invading Soviets spent two decades educating the Afghani children before they invaded militarily. Invading colonial powers have often offered to educate the children of their enemy, so they will more willingly be ruled.

To aid in the attack on the faith of Utah's children, congress started passing legislation in the 1880s to remove religious texts from schools. Too often we think the first attack on religion in government schools was in the 1960s with the removal of prayer. However, it can be traced back even further to 1887, when congress passed the Edmunds-Tucker Act which, among other things, prohibited "the use in any district school of any book of a sectarian character" *(Edmunds-Tucker Act of 1887, Section 25).*

The results were clear to those on both sides of the issue with prominent men in the community like legislator and LDS Church leader, Wilford Woodruff. He warned,

> *The perusal of books that we value as divine records is forbidden. Our children, if left to the training they receive in these schools, will grow up entirely ignorant of those principles of salvation for which the Latter-day Saints have made so many sacrifices. To permit this condition of things to exist among us would be criminal.* (Wilford Woodruff letter of 8 June 1888)

If we expect any institution to teach principles that would threaten its existence, we expect "what never was and never will be." This concept was previously not foreign to anyone and was once respected as common sense.

> *I do not wish to be governed by (others) standard of morality, nor do I wish him to teach my children. Why? Simply because I do not wish them perverted. No Gentile or reasonable man would find fault with me for that. He does not want me to teach his children my faith. All right, he can keep them away, and I want to keep mine from his influences.* (Journal of Discourses vol. 20 p 267)

For education to produce the desired results, it must be built upon a foundation of solid principles and perpetuate the values of those involved.

Elder Boyd K. Packer pointed out the effects that government schools have had, and the reason he gives seems to support the words of President Taylor. In 1996, President Packer said,

> *In many places it is literally not safe physically for youngsters to go to school. And in many schools (and it's becoming almost generally true) it is spiritually unsafe to attend public schools. Look back over the history of education to the turn of the century and the beginning of the educational philosophies pragmatism and humanism were the early ones, and they*

branched out into a number of other philosophies which have led us now into a circumstance where our schools are producing the problems that we face. (Charge to the David O. McKay School of Education, December 1996)

We're not sending our children to sectarian schools, but for many generations, we have effectively been sending our children to government 'churches' to be indoctrinated in the religion of the state.

It becomes clear in the long game, that if you can gain control of the economics, the politics and the education of the youth, you effectively control a society. We are now living with the results of the conspiracy that John Taylor warned us about.

Chapter III
High Pressure vs. Slow and Steady

We must keep re-emphasizing that none of this conspiracy was accidental and there were many organizations working together. The Utah organizations have the same end in mind, but different ways of achieving these ends. One path, like the hardcore communists use, is the in-your-face, violent, revolutionary takeover. The other path is more like the Fabian socialists who, like Karl Marx talked about in the Communist Manifesto, do things slowly, one small step at a time. The first organizations in Utah took the more aggressive approach. Two of these organizations were the Gentile League and the Utah Loyal League.

In current history books about Utah, these organizations are not mentioned. Defending Utah volunteers have been through public and university libraries all over the state in universities and public libraries statewide seeking any mention of these organizations. After searching dozens of books on Utah's history, we have found one exception. The book "Utah's History" published by Utah State University claims,

> *Extracurricular activities in the Loyal Leagues, Liberty Brigades, sewing circles, and similar youth clubs would, it was hoped, bind them to Protestantism.* (Utah's History, Richard Douglas Poll, Utah State University, pg. 328)

According to this University publication, the "Loyal League" was just a youth group. However, when you refer to earlier histories, you see a much different picture:

> *The purpose of the Loyal League was to eradicate by peaceable means, but lawful force, the doctrine of the Mormons.* (Utah Historical Quarterly, 1960, vol. 29, no. 2 pg. 148)

Going back even further to contemporary accounts of the organization, we find an even clearer picture:

> *The objects of the Utah Loyal League are to combine the loyal people of Utah… in opposition to the political rule and law-defying practices of the so-called Mormon Church* (The Saints Herald, 1 January 1887, pg 69)

Dystopian novelist, George Orwell, is credited with saying,

> *The most effective way to destroy people is to deny and obliterate their own understanding of their history.*

Modern attempts at destroying our understanding of our history have been quite successful because most of us are unaware that we are being attacked.

The other organization using more forceful tactics was the "Gentile League." No modern history book that we have come across even mentions this highly influential group from the late 1800s. "History of Utah" by Orson Hyde tells us about the secret society known as the Gentile League of Utah:

> *Under cover of 'arming and organizing for protection,' the secret society known as the 'Gentile League of Utah' was formed. Within its program (if statements from its own side may be relied upon) was the deliberate massacre of municipal officers and citizens. Such a purpose, it is said, was really conceived, and only awaited an opportunity for its execution.*
>
> *That opportunity, it was hoped by the leaders of the league, would be afforded at the election. Associated with the work and purpose of this lawless organization were leading federal officials, and prominent at public meetings where its power and purposes were boasted of, were such men as Judge Strickland, General Maxwell, R.N. Baskin, J.M. Orr, Rev. Norman McLeod, and other anti-Mormon radicals. At a meeting on East temple Street, in from of the Salt*

This was not some fringe group with limited membership. This influential organization had over two thousand members statewide. Even today, an organization with two thousand members would be a sizable organization. In the 1800s, an organization of this number is even more impressive when accounting for the difference in population. Those that made up the bulk of this organization held high positions of authority in government, such as mayors and judges. Robert Newton Baskin, who we mentioned earlier, and Federal Judge William Hayden, declared in the quote above that if their program was interrupted, the streets of Salt Lake would be seen running down with blood!

However, the conspiracy realized that they were helping the Saints stand strong for their beliefs as sometimes happens when a group bands together in opposition to an enemy. Realizing this, the conspiracy began a new approach.

Enemies Within

In October of 1869, Vice President of the united States, Schuler Colfax, came to Utah and spoke to some prominent individuals throughout the state. He came to ask, "should the feds invade Utah with troops a second time to get the Mormons in line?"

Colfax was what was called a "Radical Republican." Radical Republicans controlled congress during the 1860s and were a faction of the Republican party from the 1850s to the 1870s. They were rabid anti-Mormons and one of Lincoln's secretaries, John Hay, referred to the radical leaders in the Republican Congress as the Jacobin Club, linking them to the Illuminati. Additionally, the Radical Republicans had begun implementing just about every aspect of The Communist Manifesto's ten planks for communizing a country. A prominent Radical Republican, Senator Charles Sumner, openly advocated for a world government and court, and would ultimately join the communist organization, First International. *(See 'To the Victors Go the Myths & Monuments', Arthur R. Thompson, American Opinion Publishing, 2016)*

One of the people that Colfax visited when he came to Utah was a guy by the name of William Godbe. Godbe was a convert to the Church from

England who called himself a "Robert Owen Mormon." Nobody today would even consider calling themselves a "Robert Owen Mormon" because they do not even know who Robert Owen was.

Robert Owen is the true founder of modern-day communism. He was the one that trained Karl Marx and Frederick Engels before they wrote the Communist Manifesto. When you read the history of the church, you will read about how Joseph Smith went to a lecture on socialism and he did not believe the doctrine *(History of the Church Jesus Christ of Latter-day Saints, Smith, Vol. 6:33).* This lecture was given by a follower of Robert Owen.

Owen himself was the protégé of Madam Helena Blavatsky, the founder of the "Lucifer Trust" which later became the "Lucius Trust" and is known today as the "Theosophical Society," the brain trust of the modern New Age movement.

In addition to his New Age Socialist beliefs, Godbe was also into the occult. His home was a gathering place for what was referred to as "spiritualism." In the Autumn of 1868, Godbe and his associate, Elias Harrison, went to New York instead of attending the Church's General Conference to receive "spiritual guidance." The trip started with a visit to a well-known spiritualist and "medium,"

Charles H. Foster, who was also a professional medium for Abraham Lincoln and Andrew Johnson. When Foster greeted Godbe and Harrison, he did so in the supposed voice of Heber C. Kimball, Brigham Young's recently deceased councilor,

> *How do you do, Brother William?*
>
> *How do you do, Brother Eli?*
>
> (O.H. Conger letter, reprinted in the Salt Lake Tribune, 12 November 1879, pg. 2)

Godbe and Harrison regularly visited Foster during their three-week trip to New York to receive advice from "Kimball" (whether an evil spirit or Foster pretending, it is difficult to ascertain), whom they had admired. Godbe and Harrison received ongoing instruction through Foster on "higher" doctrines in sessions that would usually last around two hours, and claimed to be taught,

> *The laws governing the science of revelation, the facts of another life, and the philosophy or doctrine which should govern the Church of Zion.* (Mormon Tribune, 26 February 1870, pg. 69)

Godbe and Harrison were told to share these things with the world, putting themselves and this medium above the duly ordained officers in Zion.

Additionally, they claimed to have received "revelations" from Jesus Christ, Joseph Smith, Solomon, the early apostles Peter, James, and John, and from the German socialist and naturalist, Alexander Humboldt.

Ironically, these spirits told the pair that the Doctrine and Covenants could not be fully trusted. These spirits also did not like Brigham Young nor the concept of Zion. The spirits told them that Joseph Smith was simply a medium whose revelations were inferior to what they were now receiving. "Mormonism" had been started for a grand and glorious purpose, but they had now, essentially, "graduated" beyond. But because of its foundations, members could be molded to their newfound "light."

When the Vice President of the united States came to Utah the following year, it was known to Colfax that William Godbe was someone that could be of help to him to get the Mormons to comply with the dictatorial decrees passed by congress.

Understanding that a drastic action, such as another invasion, would hurt his efforts, Godbe advised Vice President Colfax to consider a "conservative, peaceful, [and] necessarily slow" reformation from within. Utahns, they assured Colfax, would work against Utahns, and Godbe and his associates would lead the way. *(See Edward Tullidge, History of Salt Lake City, pg 398)*

Godbe had essentially convinced Vice President Colfax against a forceful invasion and told him to "allow me to undermine things from within because that is going to be much more effective. When you go after the members, they stand strong, and they stand together. But when we do these things under the table, then we can be much more effective."

Colfax left Utah, letting Godbe work his plan. Godbe and Harrison formed a newspaper called Utah Magazine which later became the Mormon Tribune, and eventually what we know today as the Salt Lake Tribune, to assist in their nefarious efforts. *(See Wayward Saints: The Social and Religious Protests of the Godbeites against Brigham Young, Ronald W. Walker, BYU Studies, 2012)*

Joseph Fielding Smith later had this to say about this newspaper:

> *It had been justly said of this sheet that it was brought into the world to lie and was true to its mission.* (Essentials in Church history, page 447)

Godbe and his followers, later referred to as Godbeites, were dedicated to ending economic independence, opposing United Order efforts, stopping the rule of the Kingdom of God, and they worked hard to bring metropolitan (city) values to Utah. In short, they sought to turn Zion into Babylon.

Because of Godbe's efforts to undermine ecclesiastical leaders publicly and repeatedly, the scriptures and the building of Zion, he and Harrison were excommunicated in October of 1869. During his membership trial, Godbe attempted to defend his "freedom of speech" (of which no one ever challenged) to distract from the fact that he was openly working to assist the enemies of the Kingdom. It was honored that anyone could say what they wished, however they could not continue to undermine the private institution they were a part of and maintain fellowship.

Godbe addressed the accusations that he was a "spiritualist" by arguing,

> *We do believe in revelation but such only as comes through the channels of the Holy Priesthood and we do not believe in the teachings of spiritualism.* (October 25, 1869; Salt Lake Stake High Council, Minutes, Minutes of the Apostles of The Church of Jesus Christ of Latter-day Saints, 1835-1893, Privately Published, Salt Lake City, Utah, 2013, pg. 274)

Because he felt he was receiving instruction from Priesthood leaders beyond the veil, he rationalized his false denial, attempting to keep his membership, and thus influence, in the Church. Godbe and Harrison were both excommunicated.

An interesting point of history that should be mentioned is that William Godbe was basically seen as the "stepfather" of church president Heber J. Grant. After the death of Grant's biological father, his mother worked for Godbe, and they lived in Godbe's home. So, it is no surprise that in 1902 when William Godbe died, Heber J. Grant wrote a eulogy which said,

> *I never knew a more generous bigger-hearted or more faithful man* (Wayward Saints: The Social and Religious Protests of the Godbeites against Brigham Young, Ronald W. Walker, BYU Studies, 2012, pg. 109)

When looking at how events played out in the coming decades, it may be useful to consider that Heber J. Grant knew the apostles and was an apostle himself. Despite knowing Brigham Young, John Taylor, Wilford Woodruff, etc., he still thought so highly of William Godbe to call him "more faithful" than anyone else he knew.

A Kinder, Gentler Conspiracy

An organization was formed in 1883 that exists to this day, and its strategy has proven far more effective than the more full-frontal approach.

The Alta Club, in their autobiography, tells us that they were formed for the purpose of allowing gentiles to build businesses and business relationships in a Mormon dominated climate while keeping out of politics,

> *It was just a social club which always stuck firmly to its original purpose of being social, that it never took sides on any issue. It neither advocated nor opposed public causes...* (The Alta Club, O.N. Malmquist, The Alta Club, 1974, pg. vii)

When we came across this, we were reminded of how the Council on Foreign Relations (CFR) talks about themselves. They say that they are a "non-partisan think tank" (keeping out of politics) while they are actively trying to build world government and strengthen the United Nations. With this interesting autobiographical description of themselves piquing our interest, we looked deeper.

In 1895, Utah was holding the state's constitutional convention to write the state's constitution in preparation for joining the united States as the 45th state. To ensure the Church's interests were represented in the state Constitution, the Church of Jesus Christ of Latter-day Saints sent Apostle John Henry Smith to the convention.

Fellow apostle, Heber J. Grant, met with Smith during the convention and naming the Alta Club by name said,

> *The Alta Club having agreed to work against it [woman's suffrage] and that they proposed to use their influence to defeat the Constitution if equal suffrage were made a part of it.* (The Diaries of Heber J. Grant, 1880-1945 Abridged, Privately Published, Salt Lake City Utah, 2013, page 162)

The Alta Club's claim in having no agenda to support or oppose public causes is completely false. In fact, when you read further in their autobiography, they admit what the real agenda of their organization is. They say,

> *...the Alta Club played important roles in diminishing the bitterness of the conflict [between the Church and the world/government] to a point which permitted the territory to become a state and to function politically under the national system.* (The Alta Club, O.N. Malmquist, The Alta Club, 1974, pg. viii)

Their goal is to change every unique trait of Utah's people which might separate us from the world (their New World Order), in order to merge us politically and culturally. This agenda applies to the people of Utah whether they're a part of the LDS church or not. Utahns overwhelmingly have never believed in the doctrines of their New World Order.

As previously discussed, there are members of these organizations that have no idea what the real agenda is. This also applies to the Alta Club. The organization has levels within levels. Bottom level members of the Alta Club, often think they're just there to make friends and build business relationships, but the higher up one rises in the organization, the more he might see and become a part of the ultimate agenda.

Members of the club have repeatedly worked to bring in agendas (that we'll discuss later) by renaming ideas that would normally be unpopular. They rename and re-phrase these unpopular ideas to sound more like "the Utah way", even though it always leads to the state adopting traditionally unpopular policies.

Chapter IV

Understanding History to Understand Today

To understand how the conspiracy works today we just have to look at history. Satan does not have any new ideas because the old ideas work so well. In the book of Helaman, found in the Book of Mormon, we read that the conspirators of their day,

> [D]id unite with those bands of robbers, and did enter into their covenants and their oaths, that they would protect and preserve one another in whatsoever difficult circumstances they should be placed, that they should not suffer for their murders, and their plundering, and their stealings. (Book of Mormon, Helaman 6:21)

This shows us how the Secret Combinations operate. They conspire to protect each other for murdering, stealing, and plundering. They are protected in their crimes because they, in turn, protect their buddies in their crimes!

One clear modern example of this was when Cleon Skousen was the chief of police in Salt Lake City between 1956 to 1960. In 1960, J. Bracken Lee was elected mayor of Salt Lake City. Soon after being elected, he told Skousen not to investigate illegal activity going on at the Alta Club.

Lee was a regular at "strip-tease clubs" and gambling halls in the city and did not want to be caught attending them. Skousen refused not to enforce the law and raided an illegal poker club at which the mayor was in attendance. Skousen was then promptly fired.

Skousen supporters interrupted city council meetings and even burned crosses on the mayor's lawn in defiance of the mayors' conspiratorial actions. *(See Utah Historical Quarterly, Utah Historical Society, Fall 1974, Vol 42, No. 4, p. 332. Also, recollections of personal conversations between Skousen and Brian Mecham, founder of the website www.latterdayconservative.com)*

This is a prime modern example of the conspiracy protecting each other, and themselves, in their crimes.

As part of our investigation into the organization, independent journalists visited the Alta Club and asked if they would be willing to give a tour of the building. At the front desk was a young woman in her early twenties who agreed to give us a tour.

At one point in the tour, we were in a hallway where there was a painting on the wall of a man on his knees begging this woman for forgiveness. One journalist made the comment, "Oh man! He must have gotten in trouble and done something really bad!" The young woman giving the tour nonchalantly replies, "Oh, he probably got caught with a prostitute," and then pointed to an outside door in the hallway and says, "And that's where they sneak them in, to this day."

In fact, their own autobiography talks about their involvement in organized crime.

> *The group's contact with the so-called "underworld" was a man with the nickname of Ed.* (The Alta Club, O.N. Malmquist, 1974, pp. 48-49)

Collins online dictionary defines the underworld in a city as, "the organized crime there and the people who are involved in it."

At this point in time, the contact, the liaison between the underworld and the Alta Club, was a guy with the nickname of Ed. When Ed dies, Ed's replacements come to the Alta Club leadership and ask for three things in order to continue their relationship. First: they ask for a non-denominational religious leader to speak at Ed's funeral. Second: the mayor of Salt Lake must attend. And third: the governor of Utah must also attend Ed's funeral.

The leaders of the Alta Club agreed and provided those things so they could continue to benefit from their relationship with the criminal "underworld."

The Alta Club having been formed in 1883, let's fast forward to 1983 when 'Town and Country' magazine had been publishing articles on different cities across the country. In August of 1983, they published an article on Salt Lake City, specifically on *who you want to know* if you're a mover and shaker. A big name on their list was the mayor of Salt Lake, Ted Wilson. Today he is a part of UCARE and the Southern Utah Wilderness Alliance. Both of these organizations are directly tied to United Nations Agenda 21 programs. In the interview Ted Wilson admits,

> *Utah has a power structure that is quite concentrated, it tends to operate behind closed doors at the Alta Club.* (Town and Country Magazine, August 1983, p. 198)

He admitted that the elites, the power structure of Utah, meets in secret at the Alta Club.

How did they become the true power structure of the state between 1883 and 1983?

The most important part of that process started in 1887. A man from Kentucky, Caleb West, who was another one of the governors that was imposed on Utah by the federal government, was a key player in creating a new organization. As a part of the program of the Alta Club, we read:

Another gesture in pursuit of pacification which was supported by several Alta Club founders was the organization of the Salt Lake Chamber of Commerce... (The Alta Club, O.N. Malmquist, 1974, pp. 14-15)

In 1887, the conspiracy, as one of their programs, formed the Salt Lake Chamber of Commerce as a kind of political arm to influence businesses and legislation to accomplish their goals.

*There could be no question as to the purpose of this project and anyone who participated in it was certainly on the side of **liquidation of the conflict**. (Emphasis added)*

...Three Alta Club founders accepted places on the organizing committee. (The Alta Club, O.N. Malmquist, 1974, pp. 14-15)

When you've got these two sides, Christ versus Satan, how do you "liquidate this conflict" between Christ and Satan? Satan, of course, if he's trying to liquidate his conflict, will try to bring you over to his side as much as possible—and he'll appear to go over to Christ's side as much as he needs to in order to flatter you. That's exactly what the goal of this organization is. A real, clear, modern-day example of this can be found on our website, in an article titled "Selling Out Your

Freedoms, Businesses at Salt Lake Chamber Want Forced Masks."

(https://www.defendingutah.org/post/2020/07/10/selling-out-your-freedoms-utah-businesses-at-the-salt-lake-chamber/)

The Salt Lake Chamber of Commerce, as an extension of the "power center," controls the state health department, the legislature, and the governor. They are responsible for putting forward all of the programs that we're seeing attack our freedoms. If you pay attention, you'll see this with our health freedom, our religious rights, our property rights, and the rights of businesses. They are the ones that are in the public eye to push these agendas, as they were set up for this purpose by the Alta Club back in 1887. Whatever political program is being pushed by them (the Salt Lake Chamber) will be reflection of the political program of the conspiracy. The three Alta Club founders accepted places on the organizing committee of the chamber to ensure it followed their agenda from the beginning—and it's been generally smooth sailing for them ever since.

At the time of the Chamber's organization, most members of the LDS church still saw themselves as economically independent. LDS Saints were not joining the Chamber of Commerce.

One way the Chamber tried to encourage members to join was by working with the leadership of ZCMI. Zion's Co-operative Mercantile Institution, was founded as a place the saints could go to buy the things they needed but couldn't produce themselves, so they didn't have to purchase goods from 'Babylon.'

When it went out of business around 2002, it became basically indistinguishable from any common department store. During the late 1880s and early 1890s, leadership of ZCMI had become reportedly less focused on its original purpose and more willing to join the Salt Lake Chamber of Commerce. This helped reduce mental barriers among the general membership of the LDS church who viewed ZCMI as a cooperative led by good church members. Not long after the Mormons and Gentiles started working together in the Chamber of Commerce, some of these same Mormons were proposed and accepted as members in the Alta Club *(see The Alta Club, O.N. Malmquist, 1974, pp. 15-16)*.

This brings us back to 1983 and that "power structure" that the mayor of Salt Lake talked about. Answering the question, *who is this group of people that meet in secret at the Alta Club?* Town and Country wrote,

You have the political arm of this conspiracy (the Chamber), the cultural arm (The Tribune), and they've clearly invited even the church to their table at this point.

They are trying to change the culture through articles, polls, opinion pieces, all followed up with legislation in an attempt to move society *legally* to match what they're first doing *socially* or *culturally*. Since then, it's become obvious that this plan has expanded even further. There are additional programs and organizations that come out of the Chamber of Commerce to show for it. When we compare reports from the SL Tribune and Deseret News, and KSL, it's clear that they generally remain on the same page and nearly all the mainstream media is a part of this power structure. We can always look back at where it started, though, thanks to Town and Country Magazine: The Chamber of Commerce and The Salt Lake Tribune.

Now we would like to show more examples of how the international conspiracy has come to Utah in modern times. Any serious student of conspiracy facts must be aware of the organization known as the Federal Reserve.

The Federal Reserve, through a central bank, is one of the planks of the Communist Manifesto: "centralization of credit in the hands of the state." In 1913, the Federal Reserve was created with Colonel Edward Mandel House being called [President] "Wilson's brain."

House wanted to "build socialism as dreamed of by Karl Marx" and he was the "unseen guardian angel" of the Federal Reserve. He was the behind-the-scenes power broker to make sure that everything came together to ensure that the Federal Reserve bill was passed in 1913.

Five years later in 1918, Salt Lake City gets a branch of the Federal Reserve. How did Salt Lake get a branch of the Fed? In a 1921 General Conference, Heber J. Grant said,

> *I said to Mr. Lynch, then governor of the Federal Reserve Bank: "I pledge you the absolute loyalty of the people of Utah. I promised to put over any requirement, no matter how much it is, that is placed on the people of Utah, on one condition, and that is that you will give us a Federal Reserve branch in Salt Lake City... We have the loyalty, and if you will bring the bank here, we*

will borrow the money and we will do our share."
(Heber J. Grant, Conference Report, November 1921,
p.11-12)

Heber J. Grant brought the Federal Reserve to Utah.

The Council on Foreign Relations is another branch of the conspiracy, another tentacle of this "hydra monster." Their goal, they say, is to maintain and gradually increase the authority of the United Nations *(see CFR Study #7, 1959)* and to build the New World Order. They published an article in 2017 called 'World Order 2.0.' Remember that its co-founder, Colonel Edward Mandel House, wanted to "build... communism as dreamed of by Karl Marx."

The Council on Foreign Relations was formed after World War I, in 1921. The major motive for the political orchestration of the events that led to World War I was that this global conspiracy wanted a global catalyst to build world government. Because of this war, they introduced the League of Nations. But, thanks to good people like J. Reuben Clark Jr. who warned the people about the dangers of the League of Nations, the American people refused, and the League of Nations was stopped. People like Colonel Edward Mandel House and others of his ilk that wanted to build this New World Order, got together, and formed the Council on Foreign Relations to help make the American people more easily accept the idea of a one-world government. This leads us to World War II and the formation of the United Nations.

One of their tools to accomplish this was to form additional subgroups under what they called the American Committees on Foreign Relations. Their website talks about their history and how they were formed:

> *In 1938, the Council on Foreign Relations, possibly the most prestigious "think tank" in America believed it was time to create a number of non-partisan, non-profit Committees across the country for the purpose of bringing business and professional local leaders together to discuss world events due to isolationist attitudes and emerging international conflicts.* (acfr.org/about-us accessed in April 2021)

The CFR says that because we dared to support American independence and the Constitution, they had to start local groups to help opinion molders and business interests use their influence to persuade the local people to support the idea of world government.

Figure 4

Their map shows they have chapters all across the country, including one in Salt Lake City. They hold events every single month. What's really interesting about this is that, every month, their event is held downtown at the Alta Club. We can observe that the Alta Club is the primary organization used to funnel international programs to Utah.

We will address a couple of examples of prominent Utahns who have been CFR members in the past (not current CFR members): former Governor Jon Huntsman Jr. and Garrett Gong (current member of the Quorum of the Twelve Apostles). We encourage everyone to read our article at DefendingUtah.org called *'Jon Huntsman Jr. and the New World Order'* for more of the documentation concerning what we're going to cover about Jon Huntsman below.

In 1993, Huntsman joined the Council on Foreign Relations, and led Envision Utah (which is the leading Agenda 21 organization in Utah). In 2007, he supported Cap and Trade, which allows businesses to purchase "carbon credits" and write off their pollution. This policy is generally summed up as freedom-destroying "Green New Deal" type stuff. That same year, he backed the forced healthcare mandates leading us towards Obamacare. He backed the trillion-dollar bank bailouts in 2008 and supports forcing states to recognize gay marriage. In 2012, he attended the Bilderberg Conference and in 2015 joined the Atlantic Council, which is a branch of the Council on Foreign Relations. Then he endorsed Mike Lee for US Senate that same year and, in 2019, he was revealed to be in Jeffry Epstein's "little black book."

As mentioned before, Huntsman endorsed Mike Lee so let's evaluate some key jobs that Mike Lee has had since he graduated law school in 1997. After graduating, Lee immediately went to work as clerk for the US District Court. Just a year later, he worked as a clerk in the Supreme Court for several years. After that, Lee served as legal counsel for Jon Huntsman and then went back to the Supreme Court a year later. After doing that for only a year, he was hired by Energy Solutions. The next step in his career was being elected to the US Senate.

Moving forward with the record, we present a screenshot of a public article announcing that Orrin Hatch and Mike Lee are throwing a fundraiser for Mitch McConnell.

Washington • Sens. Orrin Hatch and Mike Lee are throwing a fundraiser for Senate Republican Leader Mitch McConnell Wednesday evening at Salt Lake City's exclusive Alta Club.

7 Aug 2013

Figure 5

Mike Lee teamed up with Orrin Hatch to raise money for this "neocon" (neo-conservative) internationalist. A "neocon" is simply a communist that believes in state power primarily through warfare instead of welfare. (For a deep dive on

Orrin Hatch's deep state connections, see defendingutah.org/hatch)

The following screenshot shows another report concerning Mike Lee.

It's no surprise that Lee has trouble with Utah's Republican establishment and it's been long rumored he'll face an intra-party challenge when he seeks re-election. Now that the 2014 elections are over and the attention is shifting to 2016, Lee and his supporters are taking steps to build his campaign apparatus.

22 Dec 2014

Figure 6

This campaign by the Tribune is complete political theater to convince grass-roots liberty-leaning conservatives that Mike Lee is getting into trouble with Utah's political establishment. "It's long been rumored that he'll face an intra-party challenge when he seeks re-election." According to the Tribune, there's no doubt about it: he's going to get opposition and it's going to be huge. The establishment will be going after him all the way. The following year, his former boss, CFR member, and Bilderberger, Jon Huntsman Jr., endorses him.

"Mike has every good intention and I say that because I worked with Mike," Huntsman told Lewis, a conservative commentator in the Washington, D.C., area. "In fact, I don't know too many people in the legislative branch who are as brilliant as Mike Lee. His understanding of the Constitution, his ability to legislate."

14 Jan 2015

Figure 7

With this endorsement, let's look at some of Lee's record:

He filed to get signatures, giving legitimacy to Count-My-Vote and destroying the neighborhood caucus system even though he had zero chance of losing at the convention and no legitimate opposition in the primary. Mike Lee sailed right into the nomination, even though the media wanted to make the grassroots republicans think that he was getting opposition from the insiders by portraying this drama. There was no opposition in the Republican party but since we are supposed to believe that "the establishment hates Mike Lee," surely the Democrats are going to come up with a top-notch, hard-to-beat candidate. They say, 'he is going to have to work really hard to win against the Democrat that year.' So, who is the best candidate that the democrats could come up with?

Figure 8

It's "Misty Snow," a cross dresser who worked for the past eighteen years as a cashier at Harmons grocery store. This is the best candidate that the establishment could run against Mike Lee? Clearly the "opposition" against Mike Lee is just a character in the political theater.

Continuing the review of Lee's record as opposed to his talking points:

- He sponsored a bill giving President Obama unilateral power to create independence destroying trade deals.
- He endorsed giving Obama unilateral legislative authority to simply veto any line in any bill that congress writes all by himself. (This amounts to granting legislative powers to the president)
- He co-sponsored a new graduated income tax legislation.
- He also teamed up with Obama to extend the Patriot Act. An article can be found on our website for more information. It was called the USA Freedom Act and had all the worst parts of the Patriot Act, ensuring domestic government spying could continue through corporate relationships. They were about to expire when Mike Lee worked with Obama to extend them in the USA Freedom Act.

- He voted several times for the national defense authorization act which 'legalizes' detaining Americans indefinitely.
- He endorsed count-my-vote by going the "signature path" (search for CMV and SB54 on our website for a full history of CMV)
- He voted for warrantless FISA taps in 2020.
- In 2022, he teamed up with the very-liberal Mitt Romney to sell federal lands back to the state with the promise they would be used only for Agenda 21 housing (communist inspired, United Nations influenced, high density housing projects).

Figure 9

It is clear, Mike Lee's actual record is much different than his rhetoric, and of course when Jon Huntsman, his former boss, runs for Governor, Lee endorses him.

Let's address another tentacle of this "hydra beast": Skull and Bones. This is a part of the international conspiracy, and for those of you that have never heard of it, we'll quote this clip from a video produced by The John Birch Society:

VIDEO TEXT: This week we look at an organization that has played a major role in American society and politics, Skull and Bones. The official story is that Skull and Bones or the Order was started in 1832 primarily by William Huntington Russell with the help of Alphonso Taft as chapter 322 of a German secret society. The speculation is that the order was the Illuminati, but no positive proof has been found that it was. Since Russell studied at the University of Berlin and Skull and Bones became known as the brotherhood of death it is likely that it was part of the Totenbund or Order of Death, itself a descendant of the Illuminati. A telling clue of their origin, even though circumstantial, is the use of the term "the Order," just as the Illuminati was known.

The other co-founder of Skull and Bones, Alphonso Taft played out a more overt influence on America by the positions he held. He became the secretary of war and the attorney general in the Grant administration. He ran for governor of Ohio but lost the race over his desire to see the

See the similar purposes of the Salt Lake Chamber of Commerce and the US Chamber of Commerce. The US Chamber works to destroy American independence and merge us into a world system like the Salt Lake Chamber works to merge Utah into the national system.

With the Skull and Bones secret society, Republicans and Democrats work together on the same goals while pretending to oppose each other in public. A search on YouTube for "George W. Bush/John Kerry Skull and Bones" will return news reports from the 2004 presidential elections where one reporter tried to bring this controversial subject to light. He asked about how they were both members of Skull & Bones, but they refused to talk about what that means and that there were many secrets that they couldn't tell. One of the initiation rites into the Skull and Bones involves the initiate lying naked in a coffin with another man to confess all of his sins. This is very occult; it's satanic and it is part of this global conspiracy to destroy freedom. It may reflect Moses 5:51 which reads,

> *For, from the days of Cain, there was a secret combination, and their works were in the dark, and they knew every man his brother.*

When you talk about Skull and Bones, everyone thinks of Yale, but there's actually a second chapter of Skull and Bones. In 1910 an unnamed Yale alumnus formed a chapter at the University of Utah. In 2015 and 2018, the school paper interviewed members of the UofU Skull and Bones order, but because they operate the same way as the Yale organization, they can't say who they are. Instead, they came to the interview with the school newspaper dressed like this:

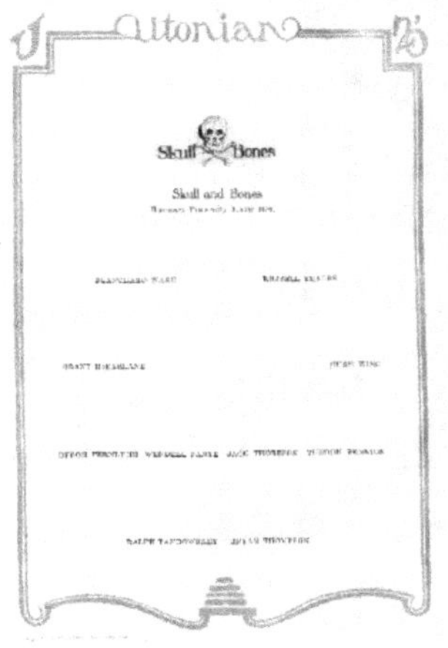

Figure 11

Some high-profile members of the Utah chapter of Skull and Bones (or Owl and Key,

Figure 10

which is the senior version), are former US Senator Robert F. Bennett, A.G. Vernon Romney, Robert D. Hales, Russel M. Nelson, Marvin J. Ashton and Hugh Pinnock. Technically, this is a college fraternity where the only data we generally have is that they were members in college. You would have to look at someone's lifelong experience to know what meaning it had for their lives after their college days, if any. For example, despite his membership in Skull & Bones in college, Robert D. Hales seems to have been a defender of liberty in his life based on quotes over the past decade. This type of research gets complicated before final conclusions can be justly attempted.

The next tentacle of this "hydra beast" is the Bohemian Club and its rituals in the Bohemian Grove.

Headquartered in San Francisco, California, the Bohemian Club was formed in 1882 and is comprised of political and media elites including Newt Gingrich, the Bushes, Clinton, Reagan, Nixon, Walter Cronkite, Jimmy Carter, and hundreds of other names of this caliber. Every summer at the "Bohemian Grove," located just north of San Francisco, members of the Bohemian Club perform a mock human sacrifice ritual called the "cremation of care," to a Babylonian owl god. To build the New World Order, they know that many evil deeds will be required, so they must sacrifice their conscience "for the greater good" in this "cremation of care" ceremony. A leaked recording of this ceremony can be found online.

A chapter of the Bohemian Club was formed in Salt Lake in 1886. It was actually the gathering place for the homosexual activists in Utah until it went underground in the 1940s. Prominent Utahn and publisher of the Salt Lake Tribune, John William Gallivan, was a member of both the Bohemian Club and the Alta Club.

Now, a lot of these names we brought up are names that are already on the public internet in this light. We felt it would seem strange if we did not bring them up considering the extensive research our team has done on this subject. Along these lines, we want to bring up something else that has a Utah connection to the Bohemian club because it's also semi-well-known: Wilford Woodruff's visit to the Bohemian Club in San Francisco.

According to a report in the Utah Journal newspaper, approximately one week before his death, LDS Church President Wilford Woodruff visited the Bohemian Club in San Francisco. Woodruff was reported to attend a dinner given in his honor. He later died at the home of Colonel

Isaac Trumbo. To analyze the situation, we will discuss the timeline of events that led to him being in San Francisco.

At this time, the church is experiencing financial trouble and, in response, Colonel Trumbo invited Church leaders to come to San Francisco to get financial assistance from the bankers there.

At this point in time (the late 1890s) Woodruff was 91 years old and recently had surgery on his intestines. It would not be a good idea, even in our day, to make an extensive road trip at that age and having just had surgery using 1800s techniques. Nonetheless, Woodruff takes a train from Salt Lake to the Bohemian Club in San Francisco and ends up dying six days later.

Some people conjecture that he was poisoned, some wonder why he went there, and some get confused again between the Bohemian Club and the Bohemian Grove. So, to clarify, he didn't go to Bohemian Grove, he went to the Bohemian Club. It is reasonable that this 91-year-old guy that just got intestinal surgery and who endured a long train ride halfway across the country simply died. It's also reasonable to say he could've been poisoned. We don't know, but we think there's some reasonable discussion in either direction and reasonable hope to find more information. With this said, we hope this gives the full context of Wilford Woodruff's trip for those that have heard this tale without all of the information surrounding the situation.

Now, let's continue to more modern times with Mitt Romney and look at his record. We will start with his time running for Senate in 1994, before he was elected Governor of Massachusetts. Mitt supports abortion, accrediting this as a passed on "value" from his parents. He also says in this same year,

> *I feel that all people should be allowed to participate in the boy scouts regardless of their sexual orientation.* (1994 Senate Debate with Ted Kennedy)

This was in the 90s. This was extreme even at that time. He wrote a letter to a group of homosexual republicans, called the Log Cabin Club, stating they:

> *played a vital role in reinvigorating the Republican party. I'm more convinced than ever before that as we seek to establish full equality...*

Because he supports cultural Marxism that diminishes the family and gender, he continues,

> *...I will provide more effective leadership than my opponent,*

so even more than Ted Kennedy,

> *if we are to achieve the goals, we share we must make equality for gays and lesbians a mainstream concern.*

He supported gay marriage even in the 90s. Romney continues,

> *I believe that the Clinton compromise was a step in the right direction. I am also convinced that it is the first of a number of steps that will ultimately lead to gays and lesbians being able to serve openly and honestly in our nation's military.*

Romney knew that this dramatic policy change couldn't happen overnight, and as we have discussed, this cultural change is done strategically in small steps. It would have been too extreme for that time, but he knew the end goal and it was finally accomplished 15-20 years after writing this letter.

In 2002, he endorsed banning guns. Also in 2002, he said that government should be forced to recognize gay marriage. In 2008, he said that God has not spoken to anyone since Moses. This was in a local TV broadcast when a newscaster asked him a hypothetical question. "If the prophet comes to you and says God tells you to do something as

President, then what are you going to do?" Romney replied, "I don't recall... God's spoken to anyone since Moses... or perhaps others." (The full interview is quoted below). Those who believed that he was a strong Mormon candidate, were sorely disappointed with this revealing conversation.

Video news report where Romney denies God has spoken to man since Moses:

> *TV NEWS REPORT: Presidential hopeful, Mitt Romney is raising some eyebrows right here in Utah. Romney was asked about God and what God might say to him or to LDS church leaders and as Chris Van Oaker is here to show us Romney's answer. It might surprise you Barb, this interview between Romney and a Boston tv station aired about 10 days ago. His comments about the LDS church didn't cause too much of a ripple back east but here in Utah they seem to raise questions about how his view of the LDS church was founded. PLAYS CLIP FROM BOSTON INTERVIEW: our next guest is the former governor of Massachusetts Mitt Romney BACK TO LOCAL NEWS REPORTER: In a lengthy interview with one of Boston's most prominent journalists, Mitt Romney was asked the following, PLAYS CLIP FROM BOSTON INTERVIEW: Should God speak to you and ask*

you to do something that might be in conflict with your duties as president or should he speak to your prophet who would speak to you, how would you make that decision how would you handle that?   BACK TO LOCAL NEWS REPORTER: to which he responded PLAYS CLIP FROM BOSTON INTERVIEW: I don't recall God speaking to me, I don't know that he's spoken anyone since uh Moses in the bush or perhaps some others. BACK TO LOCAL NEWS REPORTER: But this answer appears to contradict one of the foundations of the LDS church. In the church's first vision, a young Joseph Smith is visited by God the Father and Jesus Christ and that Smith heard God speak the following, 'one of them spake unto me calling me by name and said pointing to the other this is my beloved son hear him', and if, as Romney suggests that, God hasn't spoken to anyone for thousands of years, then what happens to the LDS church's belief in direct revelation from God to church prophets?

Fast forward to 2017; Romney reveals his support for Antifa. During this year, large Antifa riots were happening, and people were tearing down statues of historical figures. Romney says,

Figure 12

Figure 13, see online reference

Figure 13

The above screenshot of his twitter feed is describing who he believes "opposes racism," or in other words, he believes Antifa opposes racism. These were the people that he was saying were morally superior to the side protesting the violent tactics of Antifa.

A couple years later in 2019, he became the president of a secret society called the Alfalfa club (an incomplete membership list can be found at www.nndb.com/org/692/000051539). *(See Appendix B and following image).*

Romney is president of a secret society in Washington

BY KELLI PIERCE
JANUARY 29, 2019 AT 11:04 AM

Share ↱

Figure 15

WASHINGTON, D.C. — Sen. Mitt Romney, R-Utah, has been named the president of the Alfalfa Club in Washington, D.C. He has been a member of the secret society, whic includes politicians, business leaders, and billionaires, since 2015.

Romney takes over from another former Massachusetts politician, John Kerry.

Figure 14

As pictured above, KSL reports,

> *Senator Mitt Romney of Utah has been named the president of the Alfalfa club in Washington DC. He has been a member of the secret society, which includes politicians, business leaders and billionaires since 2015. This is a secret society Romney takes over from another former Massachusetts politician John Kerry.* (KSL, 29 January 2019)

In a generic search for more information on the Alfalfa Club, you'll find the mainstream claims of this club on Wikipedia. According to the wiki entry, their only purpose is to celebrate the birthday of Robert E. Lee, once a year. That's it. Their "sole purpose" is to celebrate the birthday of a Confederate general. You know, the general whose statue Romney supported being torn down by Antifa. We're supposed to believe the secret society's sole purpose is to celebrate the birthday of a Confederate general with mainstream politicians like John Kerry, Mitt Romney, and even Obama as a member and someone who attends their celebration? Wouldn't the mainstream media be asking why they are celebrating this "racist" general"? It doesn't make sense that this is their only purpose.

This secret society's membership is limited to elites in government, academia, and business. It's invitation only. If you have to apply, you're guaranteed to not be accepted. New members are only accepted when another member dies. If you want to get in, you've got to be invited, and you've got to wait for the next guy to die. It's limited to 200 members at a time and among these members are Joe Biden, Bush Senior and Junior, Nelson Rockefeller, Mike Pompeo, Collin Powell, Condoleezza Rice, Henry Kissinger, Donald Rumsfeld, Orrin Hatch, Chuck Schumer, Mike Bloomberg, Jeff Bezos, Bill Gates, Bill Marriott, etc.

Clearly, we must abandon the false left vs. right paradigm and believing that one party is good and the other is bad. This is a bipartisan game to destroy your freedom and to make you think that one side is better than the other.

We dug deeper into the Alfalfa Club. A birthday party for a Confederate general which was flaunted in the media as a secret society simply did not pass the smell test. While many of us were scouring records looking for additional information, one of our members came across a reference to the Club's autobiography written during World War I.

In search of the full autobiography, we searched archive.org, rare book dealers, Amazon reprints to no avail. Finally, one of our members found a university library in Pennsylvania with a copy. The library was kind enough to send us the scanned pages. According to their autobiography, this is what *they believe* about themselves. This autobiography was printed in 1917 and it is not in print anywhere. It was written by H. Ralph Burton. Burton was an insider with lots of connections, previously serving as,

- Special Investigator for the Senate Campaign Expenditures Committee (1938-39, 1940-41)

- Special Investigator for the House Appropriations Committee in charge of NYC and State (1939-40)

- General Counsel to the House Military Affairs Committee (1941-47)

- Chief Investigator for the Senate Committee on Post Office and Civil Service (1947-48)

- General Counsel for the House Select Committee on Current Pornographic Materials (1952-53)

- Founding Member of National Press Club

- National Union for Social Justice

In this biography, we find that members of this club believe that they're the oldest club in existence — that it goes back to ancient Egypt. They believe that they've been practicing ancient mysteries and secrets to gain the power of the ancients. They believe this "power of the ancients" has been the power behind the throne throughout time. They said it was the "Colonel Edward Mandel House" of the olden days.

Even before all the 'conspiracy theorists' revealed him, they admitted that Colonel Edward Mandel House was the power behind the throne. They believe that most, if not all, of the major wars throughout history were about whomever had control of the Alfalfa Club documents. Control of these documents meant you would win wars. So, all these wars throughout history — from ancient

Egyptian wars to the Trojan wars, and throughout time, were to obtain the secrets of the Alfalfa Club. According to this book, the Alfalfa Club put into place the leaders of ancient societies all over the world, including Japan, and that their records at this point in time (1917) were what Germany was trying to acquire during World War I. Germany believed that if they could obtain the secret documents of the Alfalfa Club, that they would win the war and become the dominant world superpower.

With Utah's politicians being invited to, and elected within, this club, we see the international conspiracy organization having more tentacles extended locally through Utah politicians.

Chapter V

The Wolves in Sheep's Clothing

To recap, in 1776, the Illuminati was formed by Adam Weishaupt and, when their courier was struck by lightning, they were discovered. Adam Weishaupt faked repentance and his inner circle formed a new organization called the Jacobins. When they were found out, a new organization was formed called the Carbonari. From the Carbonari arose an organization called the Black Hand, which we will talk about in this chapter.

A member of the Carbonari was a man named Robert Owen. Robert Owen was taught by Madame Blavatsky. Madame Blavatsky was the founder of the modern New Age movement as well as a group called the Lucifer Trust which later changed its name to the Theosophical Society. Curiously, the Theosophical Society is the only organization allowed to have a prayer room at the United Nations. Robert Owen trained Marx and Engels (Communist Manifesto). With that in mind, consider how the man William Godbe called himself a "Robert Owen Mormon" and what that means as he lived as an influential character among Mormons. And then consider how this man formed the Tribune and is a part of the Alta Club and Salt Lake Chamber agendas.

Considering all this history, what is more dangerous: the wolf openly attacking or the wolf in sheep's clothing? The wolf in sheep's clothing is much more dangerous because they look, talk, and act like your average neighbor in Utah. You're more inclined to trust them. This is why the Savior warned us about wolves in sheep's clothing. To avoid these wolves, we must learn to recognize them. To do that, we must learn and understand their agenda. When we understand the agenda, we can better recognize their actions that lead us toward their New World Order.

The enemies of freedom brag about this from time to time. After studying the private papers of the international conspiracy network, Carol Quigley, professor at Georgetown university, wrote a 1300-page book called "Tragedy and Hope". In his book, he praised their work by saying in essence, "I agree with everything this international conspiracy is working on with one exception; I disagree with how they wish to remain a secret. Everyone should know about what they're doing." In this book, he explains that one of the ways they get away with how they implement their program is that,

> *The two parties should be almost identical, so that the American people can 'throw the rascals*

Regardless of which party is in power, Republican or Democrat, we still consistently move toward bigger and bigger government and less freedom. We need to understand this concept, especially right here in the state of Utah. The wolves are in sheep's clothing. Conservatives in Utah understand that Democrats are "for big government," and they're not going to be the ones to fool conservative liberty-lovers. It's those in "our own party" using words we like, such as "constitution," quoting the Founding Fathers, and the proper role of government. These are the wolves that are more dangerous who have been much more successful in destroying our freedom than the ones that are not pretending to care about freedom.

We are witnessing the accomplishment of every goal of the Illuminati discussed in the introduction of this book:

1. Obliteration of Christianity
2. Promotion of Sensuality
3. Taking Away of Private Property
4. Abandonment of all Religion and Morality
5. Rejection of Marriage

6. Government Take Over of Parenting
7. Business Licensing
8. Wrecking of Civilization and Giving Over of Society to General Plunder (taxing)
9. Political Degeneracy
10. Manipulation of the people's thinking
11. Promotion and committing evil for the sake of evil

In 1798, Professor John Robison of the University of Edinburgh, wrote the book 'Proofs of a Conspiracy.' Several of our Founding Fathers read this book, including John Adams who wrote letters to his wife recommending the book to her and others. John Jay, the first Chief Justice of the Supreme Court, was the head of the New York committee to expose conspiracy. They knew what we were facing and they were not afraid to confront it, unlike today where the word "conspiracy" is a word that people think twice about before uttering in a serious conversation.

Presently, the The Council on Foreign Relations publishes a quarterly magazine called 'Foreign Affairs,' in which they publish their recent and upcoming efforts. We can read this to find out the mind of this conspiracy. In Utah, we have a similar publication online called 'Utah Policy.'

A few years ago, Utah Policy published an article called, "Bacon, Guns and the Buckshot Caucus, Who Really Runs GOP Politics in Utah?" In this article, we read,

> *UtahPolicy is told that members of the GOP "Illuminati" Buckshot Caucus are at it again inside the Utah Legislature.* (UtahPolicy.com 21 February 2017)

The word "Illuminati" is a hyperlink to the Wikipedia page for the Illuminati telling the reader clearly what they're referring to. The article continues,

> *The 170-member group is made up of Establishment Republican insiders, both officeholders, staff and lobbyists, among others. They have their own logo and lapel pin.* (ibid.)

Figure 16

Before Defending Utah's work exposing the Buckshot Caucus, they openly used the hashtag #UTIlluminati. Known members of this group include the former head of the Utah Republican party, Robert Anderson, Amy Winder Newton, John Dougal, and Todd Weiler. When these legislators or lobbyists or anyone, as members of this organization, use the hashtag #UTIlluminati they're bragging about who they are.

The co-founder of the Buckshot Caucus is a man by the name of Carl Downing. At the time of the Utah Policy article, his profile description on his public Facebook page included, "who knows how this **** **** black hand moves inside the halls of power" (quoted exactly, including the stars). Interestingly, this is exactly how the Utah Policy magazine article ended: "who knows how this buckshot caucus black hand moves inside the halls of power."

They call themselves the Utah Illuminati which can be dismissed as a joke, but they give another sign; another token of who they are. They need to identify themselves amongst each other and that is where the Black Hand comes in to play. It is a direct subsidiary of the Bavarian Illuminati whose constitution was based off of the Illuminati Constitution. This secret society was behind the assassinations that led to World War I, including the Assassination of Duke Ferdinand. The Buckshot named themselves Illuminati and then used the term "the Black Hand" as a more obscure reference to the same Bavarian Illuminati.

Carl Downing, is officially a registered Republican and works closely with Republican politicians. Discussing the state of Utah, this is a public thread between him and another Twitter user:

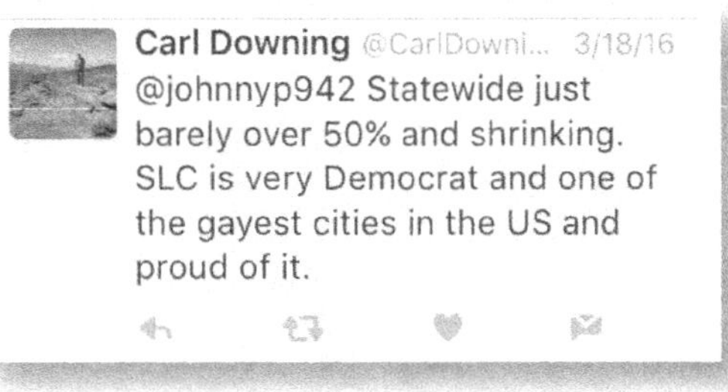

Figure 17

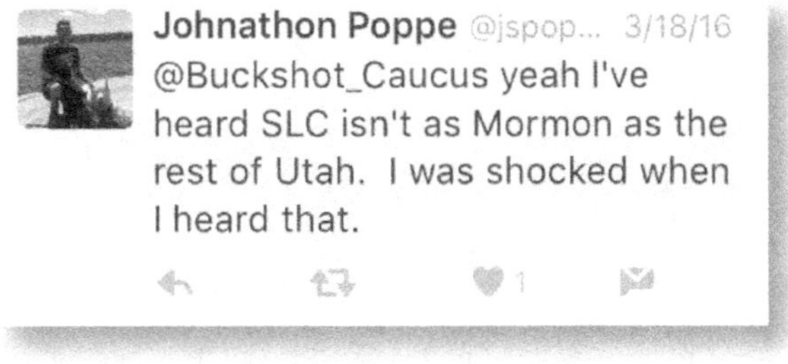

Figure 18

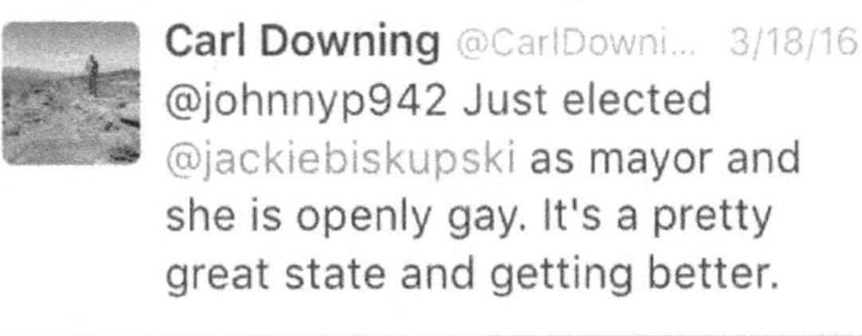

Figure 19

This "Republican party activist" that pretends to be supporting gun rights and conservative-Republican positions believes it's great that our culture is becoming conservative.

We need a proper diagnosis of the enemy. We must understand that it is not just one party versus the other—that we are facing a real conspiracy, run by people on both "sides of the aisle." When we started exposing the Buckshot Caucus, they would downplay it and make fun of our conclusions. However, eventually the response changed. Commenting on a Defending Utah article, the former Cache County Republican Party Chairman, said,

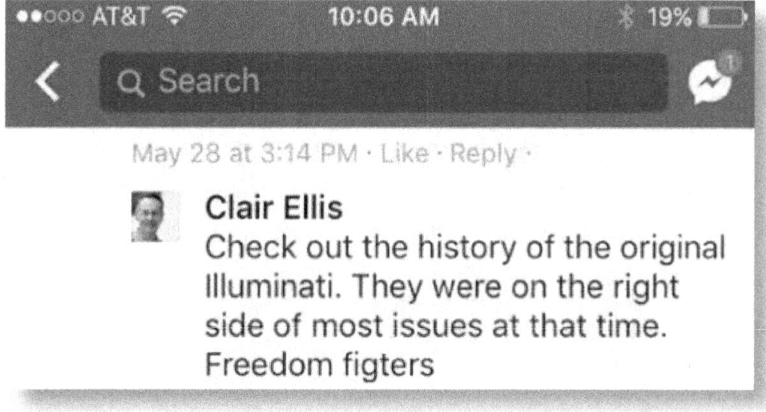

Figure 20

He actually defends this Satanic organization as "freedom fighters."

This is not about politics. This is a battle between Christ and Satan. We must recognize this and avoid the left/right paradigm that has fooled us into unknowingly supporting evil.

We don't share this information to ensure we are "the most informed people in the concentration camp" as and old JBS saying goes. There is no value in this information if it does not inspire action. Our hope is to inform, inspire and recruit others in the eternal fight for freedom. As the Apostle James tells us,

> *We are to be doers of the word and not hearers only.* (James 1:22)

Moroni implores us to "awake to a sense of your awful situation, because of this secret combination which shall be among you" and warns us to "suffer not that these murderous combinations shall get above you... even the sword of the justice of the Eternal God shall fall upon you, to your overthrow and destruction if ye shall suffer these things to be." The consequences are clear if we refuse to act (see Ether 8:19-26). However, if you don't understand the conspiracy, you will not be effective. Moroni says the reason he told us about these things is "so that evil may be done away". So, we know the end result Moroni wanted by him sharing this information with us.

Beware of arguments such as: "it's prophecy, so there's nothing we can do about it," and "Jesus will fix everything when he returns, so we just need to sit and wait." Well, why are we told about these things? Why are we told to not allow them to get above us, if there's nothing we can do about it? Clearly there's something that we're commanded to do about it. In fact, Ezra Taft Benson explained,

> *The Lord has declared that __before__ __the second__ __coming of Christ__ it will be necessary to 'destroy the secret works of darkness' in order to preserve the land of Zion — the Americas. [emphasis added]* (General Conference, Sept. 1961)

This is something that we're a part of in preparing for a future world where freedom is protected for all mankind — whether you believe you're preparing for the second coming of Christ or if you just want to be a part of establishing freedom in the tradition of the founding fathers on this earth for future generations. Religious and irreligious can unite on the principles of protecting life, liberty and property for all. We're not supposed to be merely bystanders, protecting our horde of food storage, waiting for the world to collapse around us until we can pridefully announce that "we told you so." We are here to help destroy the power of these secret combinations and to preserve what is good and build even more of that good, whether you call it Zion or just call it a free world where people are not subject to tyranny of any kind. John Taylor taught,

 (Government of God, pg. 100)

Destroying these secret combinations means neutralizing their influence and therefore their power; freedom that rises as a result is the foundation where freedom for all can thrive and Zion can be built. Defending Utah was formed to help accomplish these goals. When you're not afraid to call out the conspiracy as a conspiracy, you can be successful. Here are a few examples from Defending Utah:

- ✓ Defended 2nd Amendment & freed a man through jury nullification

- ✓ Helped parents protect their fifth amendment rights by exposing the state's vaccination opt out form admission of guilt statement

- ✓ Forced legislature to change wording on vaccine opt out form

- ✓ Stopped Obamacare expansion

- ✓ Stopped the creation of a vaccination database

- ✓ Caused a legislator craftily promoting Agenda 21 to be fired from his advocacy organization (American Lands Council) and removed from his committee chairmanship

✓ The #1 Utah based liberty organization on YouTube

✓ Only victory in Count My Vote/SB54 battle

✓ Opened businesses during the shut-down and protected businesses against illegal mandates

✓ Our own radio show & access to many other radio shows across the state

✓ Endorsed by the Finicum family, One Cowboys Stand for Freedom, Liberty Rising, LDS Conservative, Dr. Scott Bradley, Kate Dalley, Duchesne City Council members & many more

✓ Various members, inspired by principles, elected to city councils in multiple cities (on their own time)

✓ Led and organized over half a dozen organizations to stop legislation attacking the powers of Sheriffs

We need your help! Please visit defendingutah.org and click the "Learn" tab to arm yourself with the knowledge you will need to help us restore liberty in Utah. We also encourage you to become a member for access to additional resources and direct action-items to successfully resist the conspiracy and protect our constitutional government, that protects all people in their rights, as the founders originally gave it to us. Take an active role in the fight to protect life, liberty and property for current and future generations of Utahns.

<u>Appendix A</u>

Scans provided of out-of-print material to show references

DESERET BOOK COMPANY
COMMUNISM:
A statement of the
position of The
Church of Jesus Christ
of Latter-day Saints

Figure 21

A statement by President David O. McKay
concerning the position of
The Church of Jesus Christ of Latter-day Saints
on Communism.

In order that there may be no misunderstandings by bishops, stake presidents, and others regarding members of the Church participating in nonchurch meetings to study and become informed on the Constitution of the United States, Communism, etc., I wish to make the following statements that I have been sending out from my office for some time and that have come under question by some stake authorities, bishoprics, and others.

Church members are at perfect liberty to act according to their own consciences in the matter of safeguarding our way of life. They are, of course, encouraged to honor the highest standards of the gospel and to work to preserve their own freedoms. They are free to participate in nonchurch meetings that are held to warn people of the threat of Communism or any other theory or principle that will deprive us of our free agency or individual liberties vouchsafed by the Constitution of the United States.

The Church, out of respect for the rights of all its members to have their political views and loyalties, *must maintain the strictest possible neutrality*. We have no intention of trying to interfere with the fullest and freest exercise of the political franchise of our members under and within our Constitution, which the Lord declared he established "by the hands of wise men whom [he] raised up unto this very purpose" (D&C 101:80) and which, as to the principles thereof, the Prophet Joseph Smith, dedicating the Kirtland Temple, prayed should be "established forever." (D&C 109:54.) The Church does not yield any of its devotion to or convictions about safeguarding the American principles and the establishments of government under federal and state constitutions and the civil rights of men safeguarded by these.

The position of this Church on the subject of Communism has never changed. We consider it the greatest satanical threat to peace, prosperity, and the spread of God's work among men that exists on the face of the earth.

In this connection, we are continually being asked to give our opinion concerning various patriotic groups or individuals who are fighting Communism and speaking up for freedom. Our immediate concern, however, is not with parties, groups, or persons, but with principles. We therefore commend and encourage every person and every group who is sincerely seeking to study Constitutional principles and awaken a sleeping and apathetic people to the alarming conditions that are rapidly advancing about us. We wish all of our citizens throughout the land were participating in some type of organized self-education in order that they could better appreciate what is happening and know what they can do about it.

Supporting the FBI, the police, the congressional committees investigating Communism, and various organizations that are attempting to awaken the people through educational means is a policy we warmly endorse for all our people.

The entire concept and philosophy of Communism is diametrically opposed to everything for which the Church stands — *belief in Deity, belief in the dignity and eternal nature of man, and the application of the gospel to efforts for peace in the world*. Communism is militantly atheistic and is committed to the destruction of faith wherever it may be found.

The Russian Commissar of Education wrote: "We must hate Christians and Christianity. Even the best of them must be considered our worst enemies. Christian love is an obstacle to the development of the revolution. Down with love for one's neighbor. What we want is hate. Only then shall we conquer the universe."

On the other hand, the gospel teaches the existence of God as our Eternal and Heavenly Father and declares: ". . . him only shalt thou serve." (Matt. 4:10.)

Communism debases the individual and makes him the enslaved tool of the state, to which he must look for sustenance and religion. Communism destroys man's God-given free agency.

No member of this Church can be true to his faith, nor can any American be loyal to his trust, while lending aid, encouragement, or sympathy to any of these false philosophies; for if he does, they will prove snares to his feet.

Figure 22

<u>Appendix B</u>

Scans provided of out-of-print material to show references

Figure 23

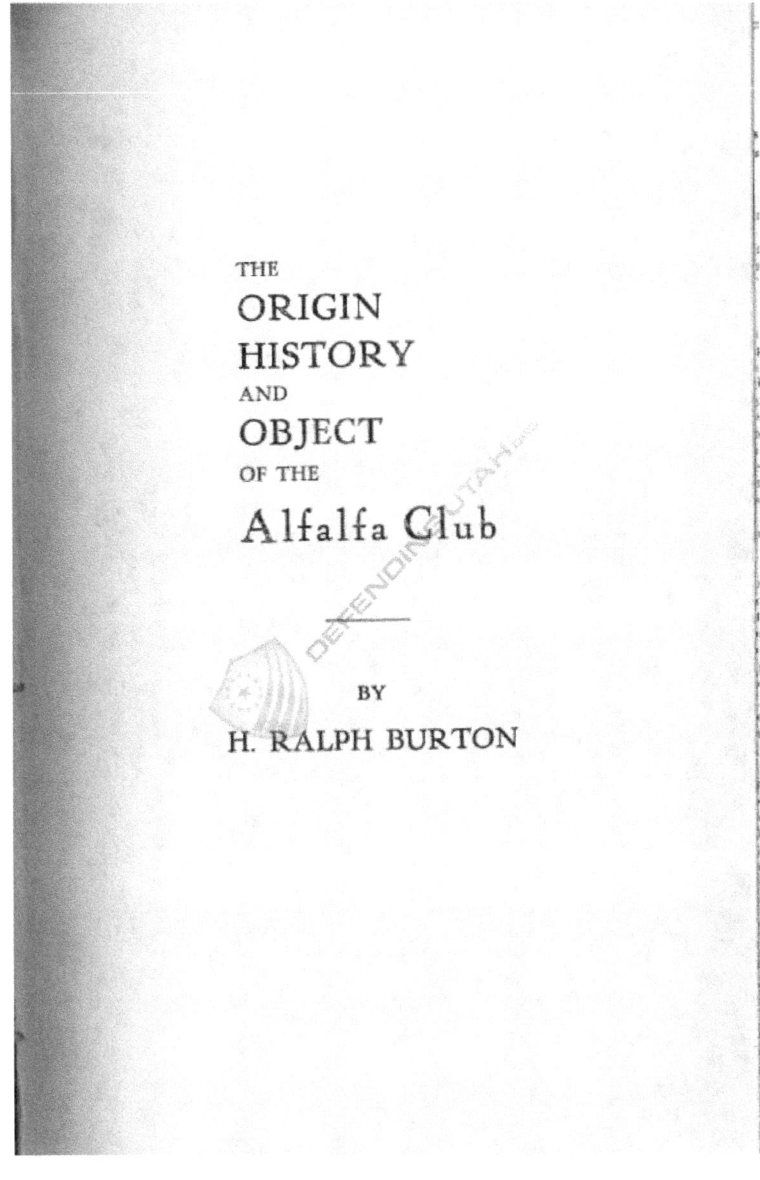

THE
ORIGIN
HISTORY
AND
OBJECT
OF THE
Alfalfa Club

BY

H. RALPH BURTON

Figure 24

The Honorable John Sharp Williams, in speaking to the Alfalfa Club on January 19, 1917, stated that to his knowledge the origin of the Alfalfa Club was indicated on the Rosetta Stone, with regard to which he elaborated at length. This proved of great interest to the members, because it is a subject about which there has always been great uncertainty. It may be of interest to the entire Club that there has been brought to my attention a manuscript which would not only corroborate Senator Williams, but which has at last given to the world information with regard to this renowned organization, which surpasses anything which the members of today could, in the most extensive flights of imagination, hardly have conceived. It gives to the Club that which many supposed it did not have. Facetious references to traditions have been met with laughing responses. Now, however, there is to be presented to those persons such historical facts with regard to this, the oldest club in existence, which should make their laughter fade as the echoes.

A man of most distinguished appearance called upon me at my office. His every appearance denoted the student, the ardent lover of research, and, above all, the gentleman. It was with pleasure that I greeted him. He asked me if he was correct in his understanding that I was a member of the Alfalfa Club, to which I replied that the happy honor was mine. Probably the enthusiasm of my response was what caused him to smile in a knowing way. He then stated that it was his good fortune to come upon information which he thought would be of great interest to the Club, in view of the great uncertainty

Figure 25

regarding its origin, history and object. With this explanation of his visit, he handed to me a package of papers, stating that they contained the record of the Club's interesting origin and history, the full description of the object, with some of the famous royal secrets being in a separate manuscript which he would bring later to the office. These interesting documents, which I have studied with utmost interest for weeks, are as follows:

There has come to me the good fortune of knowing the truth about the Alfalfa Club, which, though its members today are probably in ignorance of the fact, is the oldest known in the history of the world. Like many similar organizations, the most valuable records have been lost, although there exists today in an association of good fellowship by that name, having as its principal place of meeting the City of Washington, at least a relic of the original conception of what the ancient formulator intended. The principal source of my information was the famous Rosetta Stone, which was found by soldiers while digging the foundation of a fort during the French occupation of Egypt over a century ago. It became the property of the English, who, in 1801, placed it in the British Museum, where it remains. Part of the inscription, which is trilingual, being in hieroglyphic, demotic and Greek characters, is a decree of the Priests of Memphis (not Tennessee) conferring honors on Ptolemy V, Epiphanes, King of Egypt, B. C. 195, on the occasion of his coronation. Scholars of every nation exhausted their learning to unravel the riddle, but nothing was accomplished for many years. Among others who made an attempt was Dr. Thomas Young, the demonstrator of the vibratory nature of light. Later, however, Champollion discovered its secrets. The "Enigma of the Sphinx" was then practically solved, and the secrets of the monuments of Egypt, hidden for so many centuries, were disclosed to the world. Being an ardent student of the ancient languages, I could not be satisfied without a personal investigation of this famous work. It was for that reason that I spent months in the study of its revelations. Finally, one day, when least expecting it, I discovered in a remote

4

section of the stone, a reference to certain secret archives, which you may be sure I sought without delay. These, though they had led me into mysteries almost beyond our realization, rewarded me fully by bringing to light, among other things, the truth about the Alfalfa Club, which was never before known.

When the first known king of the human race, Menes, united the two kingdoms of Egypt under one crown, which epoch is placed by various historians from 2717 B. C. to 5867 B. C., he found it necessary to gather about him a number of real good friends, who would not mix up with the barbarians to his detriment. To this association was intrusted the great royal secrets. It was called by the king, himself, "The Alfalfa Club," which name has remained to the present day. Permit me to suggest here that it was possibly because they were so well fed by royalty that the weed we know as "alfalfa," meaning, in Arabic, "the best fodder," received its name centuries ago, rather than that the Club was named subsequently, as previously supposed. Upon the founding of the City of Memphis, and the building of the great temple of Pta, the royal archives were deposited with this organization. Mesilim, King of Kish, E-Anna-Tum, Queen Nictocrosis, Asshurbanipal, King of Ninevah, Cyrus, King of Elam, and their successors, turned to this Club for pleasure, assistance and protection. It was guardian of the royal archives. Although little known in history, it was the power behind the throne through the generations of dynasties. It was the Colonel E. M. House of the olden days. When Babylon was invaded by the Semites, which is placed as far back as 5000 B. C., it was really for the purpose of acquiring the archives of the Alfalfa Club, which they knew contained such secrets as would give them the power they desired. Mesilim, King of Kish, acquired them through the subjugation of Shirpurla, Mesopotamia, and later E-Anna-Tum, upon throwing off the Kish yoke, came into possession of these much-desired secrets. When the Chinese Empire was founded in 2800 B. C., a Western Union messenger boy escaped with the secrets, which he hid in what is now Manchuria. Later, with the assistance of Asshurbanipal, they were again

5

recovered. Hammurabi, King of Babylon, used it as a
basis of compilation of their earliest code, which is used
today by the Committee on the Judiciary in the preparation of laws for the District of Columbia, particularly
involving wet goods. When a hereditary monarchy was
founded in China, B. C. 2200, an attempt was made to
again possess these records, but without success. Its
influence was felt from 1750 to 1250 B. C., when the new
empire of Egypt attained its greatest splendor and power.
Through possession of its secrets, the inhabitants of
Assyria discovered the ingredients of mint juleps, unfortunately destroying the theory of their Kentucky origin,
which gave them sufficient pep to obtain their independence from Babylon, which occurred in 1500 B. C., according to historians. The real dope which enabled the
Hittite realm in Syria to attain its great power about 1400
B. C., was due to the cleverness of a Pinkerton detective,
who succeeded in getting a formula from the Club's
archives. These are all interesting little facts which
should make the present members of the Club feel very
proud. Rameses II, Shalmaneser I, the Phoenicians,
Theseus, the Trojans, and others successfully built their
fortunes upon the results of acquiring these secrets.

It has been authoritatively stated that when the Phoenicians, who were closely allied in language to the
Hebrews, began their colonizing career, it was only after
they came into possession of these rare archives. They
seemed to play a part in everything of consequence in
those days. Theseus used them in 1235 in connection
with the founding of Athens, the success of which we all
know. So long as the documents remained there, Athens
prospered. Right here a very interesting little story
should be told involving these interesting records. Many
such have been found in various places. We have heard
many versions of the fall of Troy, involving particularly
the incident of the great wooden horse, of which much
has been written in history. The authenticity of this has
been doubted by many. Permit me to say here that the
hieroglyphic inscriptions fully corroborate these so-called
legends. Now follows the remarkable part of it. Helen,
of Troy, through her machinations, persuaded the Am-

6

bassador from Athens to steal the famous secrets of the Alfalfa Club, which had been reposing there since its foundation. The King of Troy knew full well that with these they would be safe. The Greeks, discovering the loss of these cherished documents, immediately made warfare upon Troy. Now, the soldiers who were within the wooden horse when it was shoved through the gates of Troy, could never have succeeded if they had not known just where these documents were. The moment they got loose they beat it for the palace, where they grabbed the secrets. The Trojans were so overcome by their loss that the Greeks got the gates open before they could get a nip to pull themselves together. This is the real truth about the wooden horse. Now, there is very little of particular interest from 1184 B. C., when Troy fell, giving to the Athenians possession of the Alfalfa Club archives again, until 1017 B. C., when Solomon became king of the Hebrews. His fame is too well known for discussion. His greatest wisdom was in acquiring these documents, immediately upon his accession, because it was through them that he became the wisest of all kings. He cherished these beyond anything in his possession. It was hinted in some of the inscriptions that the great temple at Jerusalem was built by Solomon more to protect these archives than anything else. Many important events were identified with the Alfalfa Club from 1017 B. C. to 753 B. C., when Rome was founded. Evidently Sheshonk, King of Egypt, got in right with the Club, because in 973 he captured Jerusalem, after which he helped Asa, Eomer, Jehosaphat, the Syrians and Jehu, and lending some assistance to the Tyrians in their colonization of Carthage, and to Uzziah. One of the most practical things to which the Club gave its assistance was the building of the canal at Negoub, constructed to convey the waters of the Zab River to Ninevah. However, something happened to turn the tide against that famous city, for it would never have been destroyed in 789 B. C. had it had the Club's assistance.

It changes its habitat from this time, when in 753 B. C. there came to the shores of Italy, Romulus and Remus, well known to students of ancient history. It was because they had the influence of the Club and the friendship of its members, that its promise to assist in the foundation of a new empire was obtained. Without this the attempt would never have been made. The real quarrel between Romulus and Remus was not the little story about Remus jumping over a furrow made by a plow of Romulus', but to determine who was to have charge of these ancient and wondrous documents, then so greatly sought by the wise men of the world. We all know that Romulus won the argument. Hence the beginning of Rome, which city took his name.

During the several following centuries the Club was more or less inactive, although its influence was felt in many directions. It is of interest to mention some of these. A representative was sent, during the great war between Sparta and Messenia, resulting in the subjugation of the latter. The same thing occurred when Syria became subject to Tiglach-Tileser II of Assyria, who later, with the same assistance, succeeded in subjecting Chaldea to his will. Assistance was given to Hezekiah upon his ascending the throne of Judah, to King Sargon of Assyria when he conquered Samaria and put an end to the Kingdom of Israel. Just what the reason was for this is not known. Jerusalem was then captured by Sennacherib who encountered the Egyptian and Ethiopian forces and, because of some resentment on the part of the Club, his expedition to Syria failed. The accession of Manasseh to the throne of Judah was with the approval of this organization. Yamato was established by Prince Gimmu in 660 B. C. as the capital of Japan, in which event the Club played a very important part through sending a special representative to Japan at the time. Just about this time it was concluded by your predecessors that the Assyrian rule was becoming intolerable. It was for this reason that it seemed advisable to open the country to the Greeks. Moreover, there was a great shortage in shoe shine parlors, hat cleaning establishments and quick lunch rooms in that section of the continent. Therefore, in 650 B. C. the Club, by exerting its tremendous influence, succeeded in making the whole of Egypt united under Tsammetichus I, the founder of the XXVI dynasty.

8

Figure 30

It was in 640 B. C. that the Club first entered the scientific field. This was quite an event. Chales, one of the seven wise men of Greece, was a member of the Club. This has only been known since the discovery of certain records, giving the information, in very recent years. He taught the spherical form of the earth and the true causes of lunar eclipses, and also discovered the electricity of amber. It may be well understood that the standing of the Club was much enhanced through this epochal work of one of its members. The defeat of Necho by Nebuchadnezzar at Tarthemish in 605, the capture of Jerusalem by Nebuchadnezzar, the origination of the Olympian games in Greece, the dethronement of Hophra by Nebuchadnezzar in 507, the conquests of Cyrus the Great were all events in which the Club manifested its interest.

There seem to be very few references to the activities of the Club during several centuries after this; the first mention being after the birth of Caesar in 100 B. C. when many important events took place. It is very probable that, for diplomatic reasons, the Club, during this time, took very little part in events. It seems that the Club had been mixing it up pretty lively for some time previous to this time. They always were very much disposed to joviality. Apparently, they had led some of the monarchs a merry chase, resulting in domestic troubles of various kinds. This, of course, did not go well with the common people; however, they were in so strong that they soon got back with their strong stuff again.

It would appear that Cleopatra had acquired information regarding this ancient organization which had made her determined to possess its secrets if such a thing were possible. Realizing that it had reposed for several centuries somewhere in Rome, she instituted various schemes for discovering the location of its archives. It was for this reason that she first made such violent love to Julius, the Great Caesar, with whom she became very closely associated in his habitat for many years. This not availing her of what she had hoped would make her supreme in the East, she turned her attention to the honorable Marc Antony, who fell for her with a dull thud. When he, deserting his ships in battle, followed her to the shores

9

of Egypt, he was under the impression that it was his own dear self she sought. Not so, however, for Cleopatra's ambitions were greater than that by far. She thought he had the dope. He thought she was kidding him. When she threatened to kill herself it was just to make him come across with it. Somehow Marc didn't seem to appreciate the point. When word was sent to him that she had poisoned herself, he followed suit. When she heard this she let her pet asp sting her, not because she had lost Marc, but the opportunity to get what she knew would mean her supremacy.

While the records are not altogether clear upon this part of the Club's history, it would seem that St. Patrick, when he visited Rome in 340 A. D., was intrusted with the precious documents, when he started for Ireland. Apparently somewhere on the way he was caused to leave them hidden. Just what the cause for this was has never been stated. Clearly, however, he studied them with great care, because in a private letter which has been found in the search, he indicated that it was through the information obtained from these great secrets that he was enabled to drive the snakes out of Ireland, which we all know he accomplished with great success. Undoubtedly it would have been an independent sovereignty had he been able to reach there with the papers.

The only other instance in history which has been found up to the present time relates to King Alfred the Great, who seemingly owes much of this reputation of his to having acquired these documents. The story, while brief, is rather interesting. It may be recalled that there is a little story about King Alfred traveling incognito about his kingdom. On one of such occasions he was in the house of a peasant. He was asked by the lady, who left the room for a few minutes, to watch the cakes on the hearth. He did not attend to his duty very well, according to history with which we are all familiar, because he let the cakes burn, for which he was very severely criticised by the housewife upon her return. This, of course, he had to take with good grace, because he was supposedly a traveller. The truth of it is that when she left the room, he discovered, because of a loose stone,

10

157

a large secret chamber in which were hidden these valuable records which he had been devouring with great interest during the lady's absence. This is the only instance which is any particular interest until I found the documents in Germany several years ago.

This comprises all of this particular manuscript, but there was to follow in a few days one containing the great secrets.

The gentleman who called was so reluctant about his address that I did not insist upon his giving it to me. It seemed perfectly reasonable to suppose that there would not be any question about his calling with the remaining data, because he had seemed so anxious to get this to me. He seemed to be one who must be treated with the utmost consideration, because naturally having made such a wonderful discovery, he would be careful in the extreme. Several weeks passed. This seemed very strange, because he had given his assurance that in a few days he would call again. However, a very short time ago, an explanatory letter was received, which read as follows:

"Somewhere, 1917.

Dear Mr. Burton:

You are undoubtedly wondering what has become of me. You have a right to do so, because of my promises. Undoubtedly, however, when you understand my reason, you will quite agree with me that it has been the course of wisdom. One hardly knows what to do in such strange times, particularly about so important a question. You undoubtedly were impressed with the fact that the manuscript left with you stated that the documents in question were found in Germany several years ago. This is the true situation. It was with the utmost difficulty that they were brought out of that country. The truth of it is that the Kaiser depended upon these for the success of the present war to such an extent that if for one moment he had thought they were gone, he would have waited until they were found again. When it was discovered that they were not any longer in their place, the most

11

Figure 33

trained members of his secret service were set upon the trail. It would be worth my life to have one of them locate me now, for which reason I have not dared to give you an address by which you could communicate with me. It must remain so until there is a termination of the present conditions. It is my belief that Germany is now continuing the war with the hope that these great secrets may be located in time to give her supremacy. To be sure, however, they never will, unless it is for the benefit of this country, which, of course, would be the realization of my ambition. When I have determined upon a method which will enable me to leave my present hiding place, in order that I may present the records to the proper authorities, I shall communicate with you. When the opportunity presents you may expect to hear from me again.

Sincerely yours,
Friend of Alfalfa."

While the manuscript as an entirety is not complete, I felt that it was only proper to acquaint the members of the Alfalfa Club with such information as had been presented to me up to this time.

Sincerely yours,
H. Ralph Burton.

Union Trust Building,
Washington, D. C.

12

Figure 34

www.ingramcontent.com/pod-product-compliance
Lightning Source LLC
Chambersburg PA
CBHW071622150726
48000CB00004B/1836